THE
INFLUENTIAL
VOICE

Advance Praise for
The Influential Voice

"Tricia has an ability to connect to the truth of who you are and what you want to do in this world, even if you have fears about speaking that truth. What's important to note is that she will not take you where you aren't willing to go. You don't have to have all of the answers, but you have to be willing to move with her. That's what I see *The Influential Voice* as. It's an invitation to all people who have been hearing a whisper inside of themselves, telling them to speak up and speak out."

—Antuan Magic Raimone, TEDx Speaker, Universal Swing of
  Broadway's *Hamilton*, Author, and Soldier of Love

"A delightful and effective guide for those of us who are committed to crafting our big talk. With the use of real stories, samples, dos and don'ts, and even cheat sheets, Tricia Brouk teaches us how to identify our purpose, define our values, and nail our life's mission. A complete guide 'from scratch' from deciding what's an idea worth sharing to pitching the talk. Step by step. I *love* how practical this is. *This book is a must-have!*"

—Mari Carmen Pizarro, TEDx Speaker, Author, High Performance
  Executive Coach, and Founder of the International Women's
  Leadership Academy

"There is something sacred about walking through your fear and taking the microphone to tell your story—to find your voice and to share it in a way that can touch others. Tricia has a real skill for preparing you to do just that. She will help you to identify your unique message, provide you with the tools to guide you to effective practice, and coach you to powerfully share that message with a global stage. This book contains the wisdom that Tricia poured into me as I prepared for one of the most magical days of my life: the day I took the TEDxLincolnSquare stage. I wish for every reader of this book a magical day on a big stage."

—**Pamay Bassey, TEDx Speaker, Chief Experience Officer, The My 52 Weeks of Worship Project**

"*The Influential Voice* is a supportive guide for those whose powerful truths need to be shared with the world. In this inspiring collection of personal and historical accounts, Tricia reminds us of the responsibility that comes with using our voices to elevate humanity."

—**Alexander S. Vindman, Lieutenant Colonel (Ret.)**

"Nothing changes the world more than powerful stories. All of us have an inherent responsibility not only to find our purpose and our voice but once found, to share that unique story to inspire the world. Tricia has created the only book that shows you how to find it and take that critical next step of sharing it."

—**Jason Harris, Co-founder & CEO Mekanism, Bestselling Author of *The Soulful Art of Persuasion***

"*The* textbook for anyone that has something important to say but isn't sure how to go about becoming an influencer. Whether you're looking to give your big talk or you're just looking to make a difference in this world, Tricia lays out the instructions simply, thoughtfully, and realistically."

—**George Andriopoulos, CEO of Launchpad Five One Six, Author, TEDx Speaker, Executive Producer of TEDxFarmingdale, Host of The Launchcast podcast**

"This book is not just an incredibly inspiring guide to raise your unique and authentic voice, it motivates every reader to take immediate action to find their purpose in life as well as the courage to step out of their comfort zone and in front of an audience. Tricia's refreshing way of instilling confidence, eliminating self-doubt, and introducing easy yet very effective daily tactics to become highly productive allows every reader to establish themselves as powerful influencers in the world actively impacting change. If you know you have something to say but are unsure of what it is or why it matters, you will know after reading this book."

—**Irina Soriano, Head of Enablement at Seismic, Thought-leader, and Author**

"Tricia Brouk is the quintessential mentor to all those who want to use their voices to make a difference in the world. Her words in *The Influential Voice* are so powerful and relatable, encouraging you to embrace the uniqueness of you. This book is a must-read for anyone who speaks, not just professionally, but personally."

—**Lady Didi Wong, International Award-winning Keynote Speaker, and Hollywood TV and Film Producer**

THE INFLUENTIAL VOICE

SAYING WHAT YOU MEAN
for LASTING LEGACY

TRICIA BROUK

foreword by
NYDIA HAN

A POST HILL PRESS BOOK
ISBN: 978-1-64293-768-8
ISBN (eBook): 978-1-64293-769-5

Interior Layout Design: Christian Holihan

Post Hill Press
New York • Nashville
posthillpress.com

Published in the United States of America
1 2 3 4 5 6 7 8 9 10

Contents

Foreword

"I wear nice like a piece of armor." That phrase was a gift from Tricia Brouk. She gave it to me as a possible opener for a TEDx talk that I was crafting at the time. It is one of many gifts Tricia has given me over the years and symbolizes her extraordinary talent and expertise matched only by her generous spirit.

My first meeting with Tricia was over the phone. She called to invite me to participate in her show, Speakers Who Dare, in New York City. It was a TEDx-style show but cooler. Tricia had been producing TEDxLincolnSquare but decided to start her own speaker series so that she had more creative control. As a broadcast journalist, I spoke for a living, but I was trained to tell other people's stories and usually had a teleprompter. I was both thrilled and petrified by this new opportunity to share my own experience on stage to a live audience. I am tremendously grateful that my first talk was written and delivered under Tricia's guidance.

Tricia is a master storyteller and a genius at helping others identify and bring to light their own stories. She can read into your soul, cut through your exterior, and reveal who you are and what you have to say. Tricia is one of the most deeply thoughtful and empathetic people I know. She inspires you to have courage, dig deep, and find your own truth...and then express it powerfully so that you capture and even change hearts and minds. Her whole-hearted approach to her work makes for not only a life-changing experience for the speaker but for the listener as well.

It was clear from the people Tricia selected for the first class of Speakers Who Dare that her priority is to amplify the messages of the traditionally marginalized and underrepresented and those in our community who are most vulnerable. I talked about my #ThisIsAmerica journey as an Asian American and my investigation into race and racism and the diverse American experience. Sarah Nannen shared her story of being a "renegade widow" and coping with grief. Tonya Harris spoke about mental illness and discrimination through the lens of her daughter.

As someone in Tricia's show, you knew you had to meet her strict deadlines and high expectations. I remember one fellow speaker told me she had redlined his copy over and over and over again until it was finally at its best. No one minded because Tricia's purpose was clear. She pressed us so we would be heard and have maximize impact and change the world.

I am so thrilled that Tricia is helping many more people find their influential voice through this book. As I write this, our country is in a time of racial reckoning and deep division. People are yelling at each other and failing to be heard. Tricia can help you get your message across with only a whisper. Please read and let her gifts unfold for you.

Nydia Han

Emmy Award–winning journalist, TEDx speaker, and creator of #ThisIsAmerica

suburban street in Georgia. Cell phone footage had been leaked three months after the shooting took place. This kind of "breaking news" was, sadly, not new.

Anyone who watches the great filmmaker Ava DuVernay's work (e.g., Selma, *A Wrinkle in Time*, and her most recent documentary, *13th*) sees that "we the people" have always been racist. In my career and responsibly having a platform, I knew I needed to use my voice to give voice to yet another gunned-down Black man. In order to understand how I'm part of the problem and how I can be part of the solution, I decided to produce *The Big Talk Round Table: A Conscious Conversation* and invite seven of my colleagues to have a conversation with me, humbly owning my white privilege in order to inspire, educate, and inform viewers who might want to tune in. This was a small step in giving these amazing speakers a voice and collectively penetrating through noise to have impact.

My guests included:

- Nydia Han, Emmy-winning journalist and TEDx speaker, who is passionate about amplifying under-represented voices
- Gisela Adisa, Broadway, television, and voice-over actress who has studied both drama and African studies
- Antuan "Magic" Raimone, universal swing for the acclaimed Broadway hit *Hamilton*, TEDx speaker, and champion of light, love, and joy for those who want change

- Andrew David Sotomayor, lyricist, composer, arranger, and Broadway music director
- LeRon Barton, writer and TEDx speaker who had recently published the article, "Why Being a Black Man in America Never Feels Safe"
- Ming Shelby, TEDx speaker, educator, and podcaster whose happiest days are connecting with others and inspiring them to be courageous in their lives
- Tamika Felder, television producer, speaker, author, and cancer survivor on a mission to eradicate cancer, advocate for patients' voices, and mobilize others to live with purpose.

This exclusive conversation took place before the national (quickly becoming global) conversation on reform. Between when the conversation was recorded and when the conversation aired, we learned of Breonna Taylor being gunned down in her home, months earlier, only to witness George Floyd being detained by police, knee to neck, for over eight minutes until ultimately suffocating to death.

What then ensued amidst shelter-in-place orders for eighty straight days were nonstop protests. There is one universal, influential voice being heard around the world right now, and it is saying that Black Lives Matter. It is my deep hope that this combustible moment in history, an impeachment trial of the sitting U.S. president, a pandemic, and the undeniability of the systemic racism in our country will collectively remind us that together, we must speak out.

Powerful and influential voices need to be heard so they can encourage and facilitate understanding, compassion, and love while igniting and inspiring the change we need so desperately as a society. Remember that speaking your mind may encourage someone else with poignant knowledge and experience to do so also. If everyone holds back, what will happen? Silence is considered to be violence—or at a minimum, approval of the situation—at times like this. Remember that no one has your unique perspective. Bravely share it. Your words may lead to an influential decision or your own next phase in life as a dynamic leader. And we could all use another outstanding leader walking the planet in these moments.

As someone who enthusiastically specializes in voice and influence, I want you to understand the power and importance of yours. It matters, and what you say and how you say it will be the legacy you leave behind. We need you now. You have one voice. You have one life. Use your voice for good and help me make the world a better place. Let's begin.

Chapter 1

Penetrating the Noise with Your Powerful Voice

"Words mean more than what is set down on paper. It takes the human voice to infuse them with deeper meaning."
—*Maya Angelou*

KEY LESSONS

- Purpose is an ever-present aim guiding you to become influential.
- Values inform the thoughts, words, and actions that fulfill purpose.
- Mission is following a strategy that delivers results and impact.
- Curiosity is a three-part process.
- Pen to paper creates possibility that ultimately becomes reality.

I live in New York City, and the number of times an ambulance interrupts a session with a client, or a live podcast, is countless. Noise is not a low-key topic or incidental here. Nine out of ten adults in New York City are regularly exposed to noise levels higher than the seventy decibels that the EPA considers to be harmful. Noise is New Yorkers' biggest civic complaint. But I can handle the city's familiar noises as the soundscape I live in; however, the kind of noise that's polluting our world right now is no joke. We can't avoid it, and it's becoming a crisis that we need to address.

By being able to cut through the noise, penetrating it so that we can speak our truths without ever raising our voices, we can shape a new culture of dignified communication. Essentially, dignified communication is the practice of strong, honest speech that is empowering to ourselves and others. Training is imperative. We train our voices by identifying our purposes, defining our values, having a mission, and being curious.

TRAINING YOUR VOICE

Identify Your Purpose

The first step to having a powerful voice is identifying your purpose.

We have all been placed on this earth with a purpose. Not all of us have the opportunity or consciousness (yet) to use it for what it's intended for, but we all have one. You may be among those on the path to exploring your deeper purpose, or perhaps in the group distraught over the question of what to do with your life, or you're here with your natural abilities and clear indicators of your purpose as an influential voice. No matter which dot on the map you claim, it's never too late to become conscious (and we will address how in Chapter 2).

My purpose: I am meant to give voice to those who are not always heard. I am meant to give a platform to those who have powerful messages. I am meant to help give voice to those who are meant to have global impact. These voices make the world a better place by reclaiming humanity at its purest form, in turn allowing the planet to thrive and return to its genesis of perfection. This purpose statement reminds me that the person I am currently is doing the daily work to be my best self in mind, body, and spirit in order to serve my clients, community, and family at my highest level.

By identifying our purpose, we are giving ourselves a foundation, a home base that we can always come back to. This is important because our ego will try to hijack our voice. By *ego*, I am referring to the noise in our own heads that incessantly defends itself and obstructs the very goals or purposes we covet; that voice is continuously in conflict with self or others. If you ever want to know if the ego is at play, feel around to see if you're being defensive or painting self-absorbed displays of winning that come from a place of feeling threatened that isn't based on any evidence. Needless to say, you know when there is a lot of chatter going on! What is ideal for the influential voice? Philosophers and spiritual advisors refer to a "quiet ego" associated with humility, flexible thinking, the ability to savor everyday life experiences, risk-taking, and the feeling that life is meaningful.

When we move beyond a noisy ego and into quiet purpose while using our voices, we can trust we'll always be on the right track. And that is how we cut through the noise.

How do you identify your purpose?

If you have an ache in your bones to teach, to save animals, to save the planet, to write a screenplay to inspire change, to help entrepreneurs create successful businesses, that is your purpose. When you are *in* purpose, nothing you do in life feels like "work." You wake up and cannot wait to get to the things on your list. When you feel the sense of direction you are taking in your life is on the path, you've found your purpose. My purpose is to help people find their voice, whether it's from the big stage or from the big screen, so they can share important messages and help make the world a better place. (You are currently helping me be *in* purpose by reading this book. I thank you! I appreciate you.)

Your purpose is your ever-present aim that guides you, whereas values inform the thoughts, words, and actions fulfilling this purpose. Both create the power switch for cutting through all extraneous noise.

Define Your Values

Next, you'll want to get clear on your values. These are the principles that you live by. The reason identifying and aligning with your values is significant to having a powerful voice is that they will help you be consistent in your messaging and how you share your important message, whether it's on stage, in a blog post, or on social media. If you identify with any of the values I've listed below and suddenly start talking about something that does not

Ask Yourself:

What do you care about more than anything? Beyond your family, friends, and community?

_____

_____

_____

_____

Does thinking about focusing on this 24/7 get you excited? Why?

_____

_____

_____

_____

Can you tirelessly talk about all the ways you are going to be *in* purpose? How do you plan to do that?

_____

_____

_____

_____

_____

align with these core values, it will become clear to you and you can immediately self-correct. Let's say someone asks you to write a big talk about private health care and your values include integrity and equality. If you are a believer that everyone should be afforded proper health care regardless of race, gender, or socioeconomic status, you will be out of alignment in trying to write this talk. If your values include curiosity and commitment, you could write a big talk that inspires us to look at the pros and cons of the right to health care by pointing out both sides of the argument and allows the audience to come to their own conclusions. You remain in integrity while using your powerful voice to get us to think harder and potentially think differently.

Have a Mission

Our deepest nature latches onto motivation—even during times when it is a faint internal whisper. This murmur may be our mission driving us toward fulfilling our purpose.

The next step is to become clear on your mission, which will unlock the strategy that delivers results and impact. Your mission statement is a combination of purpose and values that you rely on every day to keep you on track in life, in business, in family, and in community. Having a mission will guarantee your voice is always in alignment with how you want to live your life and support the lives of others. Mission is doing what matters and outright eliminating distractions by taking action.

It was Alex Honnold's mission to do the impossible and scale the thirty-two-hundred-foot El Capitan in Yosemite National Park without a rope. In *Free Solo*, a film about Honnold's process in preparing and ultimately climbing to the top using only his hands, the vertical landscape and spectacular height increased the level of "impossibility" in the viewer's eyes. Scaling a sheer cliff face and risking drop-offs from cliffs draws the imaginary line between possible and impossible, building excitement. To call the death-defying act actually possible is hard to believe as true, even though we can watch it happen in real time in the film. But witnessing the action of Alex's white-hot mission starts up the engine internally: we have to see it as possible in order to actively pursue purpose.

Writing out a mission statement—no matter how impossible it may initially feel—is the first step to making it possible. And for all you otherwise nonwriters out there, just consider that neuroscientists have proven that writing desires and goals down makes them sear into your brain. You can actually see your mission in your mind and understand the difference it will make when executed. When we see something clearly, it changes or sparks action.

Some famous mission statements are:

- Patagonia: Build the best product, cause no unnecessary harm, use business to inspire and implement solutions to the environmental crisis.
- Warby Parker: To offer designer eyewear at a revolutionary price, while leading the way for socially conscious businesses.
- Google: To organize the world's information and make it universally accessible and useful.
- Nike: Do everything possible to expand human potential.

- Apple: To bring the best user experience to its customers through its innovative hardware, software, and services.
- Netflix: Promise our customers stellar service, our suppliers a valuable partner, our investors the prospects of sustained profitable growth, and our employees the allure of huge impact.
- Starbucks: To inspire and nurture the human spirit—one person, one cup and one neighborhood at a time.
- TED: Spread ideas.

And one not so famous...yet

- The Big Talk, my company: Being a loving and honest beacon of light and support in order to elevate, transform, and create a safe space that will illuminate the powerful stories of people and inspire greater humanity in the world.

Your mission statement needs to illuminate the importance of your purpose and what makes you uniquely different from the rest.

Be Curious (as Detective, Archaeologist, and Journalist)

The final step to having a powerful voice is by adopting the practice of getting curious. Before we can speak to anything with intelligence, we need to become informed of and clear on the "why" we are speaking. Become a detective and collect information, become an archeologist and dig deep, and become a journalist and get to the truth.

For collecting information, ask yourself:

- What do I want to talk about? (Not sure? We're going to cover mining for your big ideas in Chapter 2.)
- Why do I want to talk about it? (Get crystal clear on the impact you desire.)
- How will talking about this idea help people?

For digging deep, ask yourself:

- Am I willing to share more about how I feel?
- How will I share my personal story? (More on this in Chapter 3.)
- How will I use this information, this message, this idea to serve?

For getting to the truth, ask yourself:

- When I say this out loud how does it resonate?
- How is what I'm saying for the greater good?
- Am I willing to be criticized for saying it?

We have a responsibility to use our voice to share our story so we can reach the one person who needs to hear it. By not sharing your story, you are denying someone an opportunity to heal. When you allow the noise that's out there to infiltrate your powerful message, your opportunity for impact passes you by and you become another social media post, instead of having actual influence. I invite you to do the exercises below so that you can become clear on how to develop and use your powerful voice.

WRITING FOR PURPOSE

What am I put on this planet to do? (Be honest and go big. This is an exercise in honesty and trust. Trust yourself. Trust this process.)

_____

_____

_____

Why are you ready now to step into your purpose? (It's now or never. And if you wait any longer to step into your purpose you are wasting precious time.)

_____

_____

_____

WRITING FOR VALUES

Circle the values that resonate with you. Write down additional ones that may surface. And identify why they are your values. What about them resonate for you?

- Achievement
- Authenticity
- Authority
- Autonomy
- Balance
- Boldness
- Challenge

- Commitment
- Community
- Compassion
- Competency
- Consistency
- Courage
- Creativity
- Curiosity
- Dependability
- Determination
- Diversity
- Education
- Efficiency
- Environmentalism
- Equality
- Fairness
- Fun
- Good Humor
- Growth
- Happiness
- Health and wellness
- Honesty
- Human rights
- Humor
- Inclusion
- Influence
- Inner Harmony

- Innovation
- Integrity
- Justice
- Kindness
- Knowledge
- Leadership
- Learning
- Love
- Loyalty
- Meaningful Work
- Motivation
- Openness
- Optimism
- Passion
- Peace
- Perseverance
- Poise
- Recognition
- Reliability
- Reputation
- Respect
- Responsibility
- Self-Respect
- Service
- Spirit of Adventure
- Success
- Trustworthiness

- Wealth
- Wisdom

WRITING FOR CURIOSITY

Detective

What do you want to talk about?

Why do you want to talk about these things? (Be honest. If it's because you want to be on Oprah's *Super Soul Sunday*, you are off course. It needs to be in alignment with your purpose, your mission. How is talking about this on your *own* going to help people?)

Archaeologist

How are you going to dig deep? (It might mean coming back to this page to answer this question more than once.)

_____

_____

_____

_____

How are you willing to share more about how you feel? (This means getting vulnerable.)

_____

_____

What personal story will you share? (Be sure to have healed before you share. More on this in Chapter 3.)

_____

_____

_____

How can you use this information to serve? (And by serve, I mean serve humanity. Go big here.)

_____

_____

_____

Journalist

Let's get to the truth. The real truth, not what you think I want you to say.

When you speak your message out loud, how does it resonate? (Does it have global impact? More on this in Chapter 2.)

Why is what you're saying for the greater good? (Remember an influential voice is speaking to the masses.)

What will you do when you are criticized for saying it? (You have to be willing to be judged, in order to be an influential voice.)

> *Influential Voice Imprints*
> An influential voice understands their purpose.
> An influential voice has a clear mission.
> An influential voice adopts and lives by values.
> An influential voice is curious.

I celebrate you today. You have just taken the first step to having an influential voice. Now that you have gotten clear on your purpose, values, and mission, you are ready to identify your big idea—the idea your influential voice will share with the world.

Chapter 2

Limiting Beliefs and Becoming Conscious

ᵢᵢₗₗₗₗₗₗₗₗₗₗₗₗₗₗₗₗₗₗₗ

"If you accept a limiting belief, then it will
become a truth for you."
—*Louise Hay*

KEY LESSONS

- Limiting beliefs prevent others from hearing your important message.
- Listening is critical to building your influential voice.
- Trusting the "knowing" amplifies your influential voice.
- Your unique point of view is essential.
- Ideas must be personal and have global reach.

So many people become paralyzed when they are asked to voice their big idea. That's because they believe there are so many ideas swirling around in their mind that it's impossible to land on one.

Or they believe they have nothing new to say that anyone on the planet will care about. According to the United Nations' most recent estimates, there are 7.8 billion people on the planet. Seriously, you have a pretty good chance one of those folks will care about what you're saying.

Holding back because of an abundance or a scarcity of ideas is about limiting beliefs. These are excuses or explanations for something that may go wrong before a spark of initiative or action, not facts. Are you waiting until you're ready? Do you want to start using your voice to speak out once the kids go to college? Or perhaps once you finalize your divorce or find your life partner? Maybe you are playing small because having massive impact and success happens to "those other people"? All limiting beliefs are negative beliefs that you hold in your mind as actual convictions, when in fact they construct a state of mind that has only detrimental effects on your entire life trajectory. Try this: if you feel stuck in a belief, work on identifying the story behind it and look for the evidence that the belief holds truth. For flow and inspiration, consider talking these thoughts through with someone. And be sure it's someone you trust.

If we allow our limiting beliefs to get in the way of using our voice, the kind of change we desire is impossible. Our impact is nonexistent. And the person you are meant to reach won't hear what you have to say because you are busy getting in your own way. I state this with love: when you allow limiting beliefs to stand in the way of your powerful voice, you are preventing someone from hearing your very important message. That is irresponsible. That is selfish. You are actually withholding your powerful message from someone in need.

Just think what historical messages we may have missed by world leaders and thought leaders, philosophers, activists, and entrepreneurs if limiting beliefs had held them all back? I guarantee that our lives would be missing quite a lot of impact and choices. I want your influential voice to make history, too.

In 2019, two of my short documentary films scored theatrical release in Los Angeles. Upon the conclusion of one of them, *You're Gorgeous, I Love Your Shirt: An Inside Look at Bullying and Mental Health*, a stranger who had been watching in the cinema approached me in the lobby. He said, "Thank you for making this film. My wife and I just divorced, and I have been bullied my entire life. I was considering suicide. I've decided I'm going to live." In this moment, I was deeply humbled not only by the vulnerability this man shared with me, but also that he saw something in the story depicted on the big screen that reminded him he's not alone and that there is hope. This miraculous event is top of mind each and every day for me. We are talking about a human being choosing to live. This is the kind of impact I'm talking about. You have the potential to change and even save a life. Please don't skirt past that message without realizing the power you contain. *You have the potential to change and even save a life.*

If you are willing to stand in your power right now and become conscious with me, let's continue. But first, I want you to say out loud: "What I have to say matters. My voice matters." By saying this out loud, you are taking an oath to me, yourself, and the

Universe. And this is how you become an influential voice. Say it one more time and bask in how that feels.

"What I have to say matters. My voice matters."

Well done.

BECOMING CONSCIOUS

Being conscious means paying attention to what is true. It means wholeheartedly acknowledging the truth versus the lie so that you can fully embrace your brilliance and begin using your voice consciously. I was first introduced to the concept of truth versus lie by David Neagle, author of *The Millions Within*, and Darieth Chisolm, TEDx speaker and social justice activist, both guests on my podcast *The Big Talk* on Apple Tunes. I apply the concept generously as a daily practice and so should you. Feel and acknowledge your own existence, sensations, and surroundings in order to begin to actively challenge your thoughts and beliefs. Beware of—and look for—*typical* habits, ways of thinking, and behavioral responses that either feel outdated or incongruent with your values, purpose, or mission. Trust me: you'll know the slight twist in your gut. Call it intuition—the knowing inner voice—it's there as your consciousness, and it may be time to awaken it!

From a place of potential, lies can easily be disguised as our truth. At an early age and into adulthood, that can easily imprison us if we continue to reaffirm the lies. If we gauge limiting beliefs and lies as truth, we automatically write our lives as a limited story. This story is barren of facts and fulfillment, and abundant in dissatisfaction and conflict. Call it *The Half-Life* or *Road of Regrets*, but no one, including the author, will want to touch it because the title page is fraught with melancholy.

Early in my career, one of my lies was that I "accidentally" became a choreographer. The next one was that I "accidentally" became a director, and the final lie I was telling myself and everyone else was that I "accidentally" became a writer. My false story was full of accidents! Doesn't sound so influential, does it?

I was unconscious to the truth. The truth is that I became a choreographer because I was prepared to step into that role and meant to show up in the world that way, immersed in dance composition. I became a director, steering artistic and dramatic aspects of a narrative because I chose to step fully into my power as a visionary storyteller. And I am a prolific writer who shows up every day relentlessly to write because I desire lasting legacy through story. The truth is that my voice was meant to be expressed through movement, on stages, and on pages in order to serve humanity.

These are facts. This is my factual story.

I have been in showbiz my entire life, working in film, television, and theater. I've worked with actors Kate Winslet, Susan Sarandon, Christopher Walken, Eddie Izzard, Kelly Reilly, Steve Buscemi, Bobby Cannavale, and my dear friend, the late James Gandolfini. I danced all over the world in places like the Paris Opera House and Lincoln Center. I've written two musicals, both produced in New York City, a screenplay, and TV pilot, and I make documentary films about people doing incredible things. Most of this I accomplished by being "unconsciously competent," as the aforementioned David Neagle calls it.

I am talented, I am hardworking, and I am disciplined. A total package of competence. What I had been missing was true consciousness and an understanding that my voice carried a purpose bigger than me.

When I was thirteen years old, I competed in the Petite Junior Miss Dance competition. These kinds of competitions provided scholarships to Broadway Dance Center in New York City, where I imagined myself being someday. I saw myself in New York City being on big stages dancing with Mikhail Baryshnikov, one of the greatest dancers of all time.

I had to wear a dress for the competition during the modeling portion of the show, where we would walk in T formation, walking downstage center, then stage right and left as the emcee would introduce us and announce what our hobbies were. My hobby was collecting stickers. And I merely said that because I only had dance, but *collecting stickers*? Lame! I hated this part of the show. I hated it because all the other girls wore beautiful pink dresses and lace.

They reminded me of ornate lampshades. I thought, Those are the kinds of girls who win. Those are the kinds of girls who dance with Baryshnikov, not me. You know what I'm speaking of here: "the others" meant for, destined for, chosen for my heartfelt aspirations and opportunities. They could dance alongside my icon. I could not.

My dress was from Sears and it was gray and plain. I didn't stand a chance. I'm from a small town in Missouri named after a pig, and these girls are from Chesterfield. Think about it: Arnold. Chesterfield. They even sound poor and rich.

Then something I could not have dreamt of happened.

They called my name. "Tricia Brouk." It was as if I heard my name for the first time and in a commanding voice that held the key to my future. They placed a tiara on my head and handed me a bouquet of red silk roses, crowning me the Petite Junior Miss Dance of St. Louis. I had won. I couldn't believe it. *I am so lucky,* I thought. Here's the lie. This was my first experience at being unconsciously competent. Why did I not consider the hours and hours of rehearsals I put into the competition? The blisters on my toes from the pointe shoes? And the debilitating nerves for weeks leading up to the day? I worked extremely hard, did an amazing job, and earned the winning position. That is the truth. Being lucky is the lie.

When you identify what your truth is and become conscious of it, releasing all the lies, you will further step into the power of your voice. Neagle writes: "Faith and confidence in the universe and its laws can be accepted pretty quickly. Accepting that what you truly want and are here to do will be supported by the universe can be grasped as well. But knowing what your heart truly desires is a big question of its own. In fact, once you become even marginally aware of who you are—no awareness will have more influence on outcomes than the certainty of knowing what you truly want."

By the way, I went on to dance with Baryshnikov when I was dancing with the Lucinda Childs Dance Company in New York City. The truth? I was the kind of girl who danced with Baryshnikov.

My truth is that I'm on a mission to make the world a better place by helping people find and use their voice for impact and good. And the moment I became conscious of and living this truth and what I truly desire is when I began attracting speakers (like you) who want to have a big impact.

Ask Yourself:
  What are your lies?
  - Are you too busy to write this talk?
  - Do you want to wait until it's perfectly formed in your mind?
  - Do you need letters after your name in order to share this important message?
  - Are you mediocre at writing?
  - Do you struggle with form- ing your thoughts?
  - Are your ideas unimportant?

  What are your truths?
  - My truths for you are:
  - What you have to say matters because someone is meant to hear it.
  - You can have impact with your message.
  - You believe you can change and even save a life

REVOLUTIONARY SILENCE

The second part of becoming conscious is about *listening*. Having a voice starts with listening—mindfully hearing and comprehending information delivered from within or from another person. Listening is an act of love. Just think: we are here together cultivating your influential voice with the aim of people listening. Every voice matters.

PBS's phenomenal program, StoryCorps, records, preserves, and shares peoples' stories so that the wisdom of humanity lives on for future generations. Through a partnership with the American Folklife Center at the Library of Congress, the show is building a national archive of these interviews to create a wealth of voices and first-person narratives for future historians. I love their mission statement: "Listening to one another strengthens our social and emotional muscles and helps us build powerful interpersonal connections."

And as you become more attuned to listening, know that sometimes, you will receive answers to questions you didn't ask. This is when the power of and commitment to listening is crucial.

In 2018, I was sitting at my kitchen table preparing for a call with Grace Smith. She is a very influential voice who founded Grace Space Hypnosis and is a well-known television personality and author. As I was gathering my thoughts in preparation for our session, I heard in my head, *You have to move.* I wasn't *thinking* about moving. It was not on my radar in the slightest. Also, if you know anything about living in New York City, when you have a good deal on an apartment, you don't move. You don't even entertain the thought of it. Joe, my husband, and I had been living there for ten years since we got married, and he had been there five years before. It was in a great neighborhood, the landlords loved us, and there was no talk of moving. My first thought was, *Huh. Well, I hope Joe comes with me.* There was no hesitation, no questioning, no inkling or even question of how relocation would occur. It was simply that I knew I had to listen to this download of information.

That moment of listening changed my life and the trajectory of my work and our family. Because I was conscious and listened to a greater knowing and moved into trust and affirmation, I was able to expand. This also gave me the perfect moment to use my communication skills in an elevated way that I hadn't needed to exercise before. I was not asking Joe if we could move; I was inspiring him to agree to moving into a new, beautiful two-bedroom, two-bathroom apartment in a doorman building that faced the Alvin Ailey Dance Theater because I knew it was what we were meant to do. Asking him to trust me on the deepest of levels, entering into the space of the unknown because I could see the possibilities of our future together, was one of my proudest speeches.

This is the type of speech that needed to rise from listening. Ignoring the information that I heard and comprehended was unequivocally not an option.

Your voice is powerful. What you have to say matters, and it's not always going to be from a big stage to a chorus of cheering, adoring audience members. Remember that.

PASSION AND PERSUASION:
THE POWER OF POV

Now that you are becoming conscious, your ideas are going to appear with more clarity and consistency. And guess what? There are not many new ideas. Fact: This is not a limiting belief. If you add up the three thousand thoughts that we have an hour and multiply that number by 7.8 billion people on the planet, there's a generous chance you and a few other people are going to land on the same idea. However, there is some promising news here meant to push you forward into that spectacular idea. The promising news is that there are *always* original ways of thinking about everything. This is the capacity and strength of point of view (POV). POV is the unique way you see the world. I used to always say, "The world is round is not a new idea." However, if we both tell a story about this, they would be very different based on our individual points of view.

Do you know how many authors have tackled vampirism since Bram Stoker wrote *Dracula* in 1897? Better yet, what about *Romeo and Juliet*–like stories since Shakespeare flipped his quills in 1597? *Oklahoma!* premiered on Broadway in 1943 and had seven subsequent revivals. Many story concepts are simply timeless, serving as building blocks for a next and funkier rendition. And that's okay in the grand scheme of humankind.

Now, I consider the fact that every human being on the planet, back to 7.8 billion, has the experience of being alive during a pandemic. That is a fact. The occurrence of this is not a new subject matter or idea; however, there will be thousands of stories that people will tell about this time, and each chapter will be woven with how each writer experienced this time in history. Can you imagine the intriguing scenes we'll read about? Even New York City's starving rats made headlines! The compelling details will be unique to every author and therefore have an impact even though the plot will consist of the same topic, the same potential idea. This is astonishing. What makes you unique; how you grew up, where you grew up, what your purpose, values, and mission are, how you see the world—this is your POV.

I grew up on a small farm in Missouri. We lived next door to my grandparents. My grandfather taught me how to shoot a gun. My sister and I sold strawberries on the corner and played hide-and-seek in the cornfields. My grandmother would prepare squirrels (the ones I helped shoot and skin with my grandfather) for lunch. There was an outhouse in their backyard, and I sometimes drove the tractor for fun. In the evenings, we'd sit under a big tree with our grandmother. This was my POV.

Mind you, this all changed the second I went to see my sister dance in a recital where she was dressed as a pink poodle. I was seven years old; she was three years old. I had no desire to be a pink poodle, but I knew there was something more for me and that I was going to be on big stages. I birthed the idea in that moment that I would become a ballerina, move to New York City, and dance with Baryshnikov. And to this day, all of my ideas are seen through the lens of my point of view. I do not eat meat. I am humble and hardworking, and I prefer to stay in five-star resorts over campsites. For all you campers out there, no disrespect.

Allow your point of view to inform what idea you land on and how you talk about it. Remember the world is round, and how you share that information will be unique to you.

Let's talk about how to land on an idea.

If you have no ideas, don't panic. They are brewing within the walls of your imagination, insight, observations, and experiences; you just haven't learned where to look. Alternately, if you harbor too many ideas, this process will serve you as well. What you can start doing right now is what I call the *mining process*. You must mine for ideas until you land on the one you want to begin writing about.

Example: "Mining After Marriage"

When I got married, I cried uncontrollably the next day. Not because I had made a mistake, but because I did not know who I was. That's right—I lost my identity. On our honeymoon, I read Elizabeth Gilbert's book *Committed: A Love Story*, about a skeptic who makes peace with marriage. In short, the book is about *not* getting married! I had no idea how to be a married person. I was thirty-eight years old when I got married as a successful and independent woman. How was I supposed to show up in the world now? As someone's wife? It was foreign and terrifying to me. I did not refer to my husband as "my husband" for an entire year. I would introduce him as "Joe. This is Joe." What I came to learn was that I had to mourn the loss of my single self in order to fully embrace the new role I cast myself in. I share this because what's important to me is helping women who have not considered a big life change, whether it's getting married or having children, and the mourning period that must come along with so that they can navigate these moments with more awareness in order to minimize suffering. This idea was mined from me asking myself what's important to me and why. Oh, and my husband Joe and I have been married (with my total acceptance) for eleven blissful years. And he loves our new apartment.

PICTURE THE UNIVERSAL IDEA: PERSONAL AND GLOBAL REACH

In getting to the heart of your idea, reach for impressions that feel personal. Here is a delicious example:

A few years ago, one of my speakers approached me with a desire to talk about how he became a vegan because of meeting his friend John. They had a conversation at lunch about what John was eating and why he was a vegan (living on a plant-based diet). My speaker found this new idea worth exploring and began to learn as much as he could about being vegan. He realized it aligned with his purpose and values—and it soon became his mission. What we landed on after mining for ideas was that the way he grew up enjoying food around the table with his family had a profound impact on him. He loved those memories. These family dinners and the time they spent together helped shape him into the man he had become. That said, this story was keeping him stuck.

We kept mining and asking questions centered on truth versus lie and propelled him to more conscious thinking. Once he removed the lie that you have to have meat at dinner to enjoy family time and adopted the truth that it's the family time, not the dish, that creates the memories, he was able to fully embrace this idea that being vegan does not mean having to give anything up after all.

His idea: *Compassionate family dinners can create the same kind of fond memories as the ones he grew up with.*

How do you go from personal to global? Global may seem like a gigantic aspiration at first, particularly from that place in your head that has spun limiting beliefs and limitations. I assure you, however, that you can hit the jackpot of impact for the masses with a layering of *context*. Context is a frame that surrounds the idea so it can be fully understood and assessed. Context is designed to elicit effect, whether emotion, action, or both. The influential voice strives for both. The influential voice does not speak in small terms. In essence, we love context!

With that, if global still seems far-reaching, think of it as your talk resonating with anyone anywhere, even if you are racially, culturally, and socioeconomically different. Viewing context in these terms allows for thinking big. It's your initial idea on steroids.

Context includes these three questions:

1. Why is the idea important?
2. Why is the idea important to you?
3. Why is the idea important to the world?

One of the first speakers I worked with, Kristin Smedley, established the Curing Retinal Blindness Foundation and wanted to take a TED stage with this topic. She started this foundation because two of her three children were born blind with a rare eye disease. She started the company for very personal reasons. She also spoke on the topic for many years to solve problems, bring awareness, and, ultimately, to search for a cure.

Initially, Kristin's idea was connected to blindness and rare eye diseases, but it wasn't solely about rare eye diseases. She shared with me how incredibly proud she is of the achievement of her sons. Kristin shared that she was constantly surprised at how they both lived their lives fearlessly and ferociously even in the face of what she deemed to be a huge life challenge: facing blindness. What we came to know by becoming conscious, looking at the truth versus the lie, and by asking three questions, was that Kristin's talk was not about rare eye diseases; her talk was actually about "how she learned to see the world through the eyes of her children." Talk about context! This story still gives me chills. I can see the world through the eyes of another human being and immediately be catapulted into compassion and empathy. The sensation you may get from this talk is the urge to look at life and experience with more wonder, innocence, and imagination. After all, you were a child. Open and curious. Seeing only possibilities. Seeing only good. Take a moment to think about your understanding and interpretation of seeing the world through the eyes of someone else, especially the eyes of children, and you may just be swept into more inquisitiveness and delight again.

Kristin nailed her personal and global talk. Instead of, "It's time to bring awareness to cure a disease that's been overlooked for too long," we can apply context and go deeper. Mine it with me!

Why is this idea important?
- She wants to create awareness around a rare eye disease.

Why is this idea important to Kristin?
- She has two blind children.

Why is this idea important to the world?
- As a mother of two blind children, she saw the world as limited for them, until she saw the world through their eyes and realized the limitations were her own.

This now becomes a talk that we can all connect with; it's global. If she had limited the idea to only rare eye disease, I would not resonate with this talk because I don't have children or blind children. But I can absolutely understand what it means to see the world through someone else's eyes and have compassion while acknowledging my own limitations. Now we are talking about a powerful idea that has global impact.

WRITING ABOUT YOUR LIMITING BELIEFS—AND RELEASING THEM

What are your lies?

_____

_____

_____

_____

What are your truths?

_____

_____

_____

_____

What is your POV?

_____

_____

_____

_____

WRITING TO MINE YOUR BIG IDEA

What is important to you? (This can be as deep as world peace or as simple as cooking, spending time with family, or whatever you align with.)

If I were to answer this question it would be my relationship with Joe, my family. Family is important to me.

That is not really an idea, so I need to move into the massaging portion of idea mining. That leads me to these three ideas:

1. Laughing is my antidepressant.
2. Forgiveness is a religion.
3. Sharing must be taught.

For anyone who's been married, is married, or is in any union, you know it can be complicated, challenging, and even impossible. Still, family is important to me, so when I think about the requirement of having laughter and forgiveness in my "family dynamic" with Joe, as my drug and spiritual of choice, it becomes an idea borne out of answering a question. And I don't love sharing, but it can be taught even to an adult.

Your turn. What is important to you?

_____

_____

_____

What are you good at?

I'm really good at assessing someone's state. I spend a lot of time getting into the heads of my speakers and actors so I can support them in their most vulnerable state. When I massage the answer to this question, I get to this idea:

Speaking without words and the impact of the silence.

Your turn. What are you good at?

_____

_____

_____

How does this support your impact on the world? Being clear on what you're good at absolutely supports your impact

on the world, and it is part of your journey to becoming an influential voice.

_____

_____

_____

_____

What are you bad at?

I'm terrible at reading directions. Ikea furniture is not an option for me. If I were to massage this answer into an idea, it might be:

Why your brain needs the gym too.

Your turn. What are you bad at?

_____

_____

_____

_____

Now that you are becoming more comfortable with the mining and massaging process. And now that you have an idea...

What can you teach us that aligns with an idea?

_____

_____

_____

_____

What do you wish you could do by sharing your big idea?
(Paint a picture of what's possible for yourself and the
world around you.)

_____

_____

_____

What do you know you can do by sharing this idea? (Implore
confidence and allow your spirit of assurance to inspire confidence in others with your idea.)

_____

_____

What legacy do you want to leave by sharing this big idea?
(Think big. By reading this book, you have become part of my
lasting legacy. Thank you!)

_____

_____

_____

WRITING TO GO GLOBAL

(Choose one idea from the questions you answered above.)

Why is this idea important?

_____

_____

_____

_____

Why is this idea important to you?

_____

_____

_____

_____

Why is this idea important to the world?

_____

_____

_____

Influential Voice Imprints

An influential voice is willing to practice the concept of truth versus lie.

An influential voice will patiently mine for the ideas deep within, until they are revealed.

An influential voice gets clear on their unique point of view and is willing to share it, vulnerably.

An influential voice applies context for global impact.

Before we move onto Chapter 3, I invite you to declare again out loud, "What I have to say matters. My voice matters." Again I remind you that by speaking this out loud, you are taking an oath to me, yourself, and the Universe. And you are stepping into the role of influential voice. *I'm so proud of you. Bye, limiting beliefs!*

Chapter 3

Using Your Voice Is a Great Responsibility

> "When the whole world is silent, even one voice becomes powerful."
> —*Malala Yousafzai*

KEY LESSONS

- A through line is one sentence that captures the critical elements of your big idea and keeps you on track as a writer.
- Relatability sparks instant connection to your audience and inspires them to embrace your big idea.
- Using the technique of story arc will elevate your influential voice as a writer.
- Being vulnerable for impact also requires being healed from any trauma you share from the stage.
- Being an influential voice requires courage and sacrifice.

Part of having an influential voice is understanding that words matter and how they land on someone has the opportunity to lift them up or hold them down. What this means is that your recipient's next emotion, thought, and/or action will be directly influenced by your message. This impact is not merely about "choosing your words carefully," "thinking before you speak," filtering, or discerning. Saying what you mean centers on your intention behind crafting those words. Of course, not every word that comes out of our mouth is precise, effective, or brilliant. Casual speech is human and even superhuman. For the sake of working on your influential voice, know that your words are power—and influence.

Decide on the kind of impact you want to have with your words today and commit to it.

I invite you to say this out loud today, tomorrow, and the next day: "I commit to lifting others up with my influential voice."

Credibility, relatability, vulnerability, and responsibility are foundational elements in having an influential voice. Credibility shows that you have done the work to be the person speaking. Relatability demonstrates your desire to connect with others so that you may be more readily heard. Vulnerability shows the humanity that you speak from, and responsibility is how you acknowledge this powerful platform and use it for good.

CREDIBILITY IS COMMANDABILITY

Being credible does not require you to have a PhD after your name. It means you have lived the experience you are talking about. It means you are poised, rehearsed, and dressed for the part. It means that you use data to back up your findings and you are accurate when citing dates and facts. Being credible also means that you do not use "and," "so," "um," "do ya know what I mean," and "like." I'm really tempted to repeat this point because of the frequency I hear this messy talk—particularly when someone is delivering an extremely powerful message. They don't realize that the substance can instantly get lost with poor delivery. This is because of a fusion of what we hear as language and sound from another person that we're paying attention to in terms of their message (it's called attentiveness and interest; hallelujah when you receive it!) and appearance (someone in ad lib mode or struggling with language in front of us brings about discomfort and even pity rather than connection).

In her book, *Speak Up, Show Up, and Stand Out*, Loretta Malandro refers to "credibility reducers and credibility boosters." And you can't possibly be an influential voice if your voice is full of credibility reducers, which she defines as "words and phrases that decrease the positive perceptions others have of you and taint your reputation and opportunities. Using language to generalize or make vague and imprecise references leads people to question your abilities and commitment. If you use these word traps repeatedly, you may find yourself becoming incredibly irrelevant."

This scenario that Malandro describes absolutely cannot happen in the world of the influential voice because your purpose and mission will be meaningless to others if you lose credibility and relatability. Being credible also means that you understand your through line, convey the story arc, and take your audience on a journey. This is where true expertise and finesse come in.

MIGHTY, MIGHTY THROUGH LINE

My definition of through line is the concise, articulate, and singular progression of your big idea. The through line of your big talk should sum up and incorporate all unique aspects of your big idea without going in circles. Hence *through line.* The through line should be one sentence. If your through line is more than one sentence, it becomes a multiprogression of your big idea instead of the singular progression. And it creates confusion for you in the writing process and will show up as chaotic in the delivery. The through line is the heartbeat of your talk. It's the north star. The through line is meant to bring you back to center during the writing process so that when you begin to veer of course, away from your big idea, you can come back and be an effective author.

Here are some of the powerful through lines from TEDxLincolnSquare:

> *Seeing the world through the eyes of my blind children taught me I was the one with limitations.*
>
> How I Learned to See through the Eyes of My Sons by Kristin Smedley
>
> *The art of improvisation creates compassion in the world because we live by "yes and" instead of "no but."*

How Improv Training Can Create Compassionate Behavior by Rich Hollman

We may think technology is helping us connect but it's ultimately creating a society of loneliness

Looking Up in an Epidemic of Looking Down by Mandy Antoniacci

WRITING THE HEARTBEAT OF YOUR BIG TALK

What is your through line? One sentence that sums up what you are going to be talking about and why we should listen.

_____

_____

_____

_____

STORY ARC: CLARITY AND ORIGINALITY

Narrative arc, also called a story arc, is a literary term for the path a story follows. It provides a backbone by providing a clear beginning, middle, and end of the story.

The concept of narrative arc as we know it today was created by Gustav Freytag, a German novelist and playwright who closely analyzed ancient Greek writing with this concept, and we can also refer to William Shakespeare's five-act plays as exquisite examples of following the narrative arc. As the term suggests, a typical narrative arc starts low, moves up and over the mountain, resolving at the bottom.

Jane Alison's lush description of narrative arc for *The Paris Review*:

> We first apprehend text as texture—blurry or dense, black on white—and perceive each word as a picture (the part of our brain that recognizes words has a twin that recognizes faces). Then we pass through the words' looks and into their meanings, absorbing a stream of visual images conjured by the language. Next, we might develop another layer of "vision," sensing elements that give the story structure: a late scene mirrors an earlier one, or a subtle use of color tints the whole. And as we read, we travel not just through places portrayed in the story but through the narrative itself.

Do you see the layers of story that Alison defines? You want your arc to achieve that!

Story arcs are universally used in novels, films, and television series. In a TV series, the story arc is told over all the episodes. This kind of narrative is meant to take the audience on a journey. We as an audience want to experience ups and downs with you, not knowing how things are going to end but looking to you as the credible expert to guide us in your safe hands. When you begin writing your big talk, I invite you to use this kind of a narrative so that you can ensure your talk will have the most impact.

Story arcs can contain Freytag's five key components:

STORY ARC

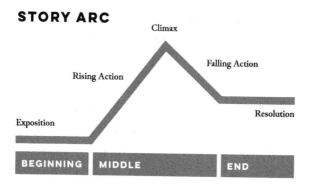

1. Exposition
2. Rising action
3. Climax
4. Falling action
5. Resolution

We will start with the exposition. You paint the picture of who the characters are and sprinkle in some detail. Where do they live? What's happening in their life? What do they care about?

Think of it as an introduction that helps the audience settle into the story before things start to pick up. Let's look at the story of Cinderella, which by the way, has reigned as a big idea in at least five hundred versions all over the world for more than two thousand years!

By laying out the details of our characters and who they are, where they live, and what they care about, we become invested in the story.

- Cinderella – A young girl unjustly oppressed, the protagonist

- Ugly Stepsisters – The bullies, the antagonists
- A Castle – Details of a future made possible
- Prince Charming – A character who may have the solution to a problem

The rising action happens after the stage has been set for the readers and begins to move the story in a forward and upward direction. (Hence, arc.) The rising action is generally characterized by conflict, usually problems and challenges that the characters must overcome.

- The Royal Ball – Everyone is town is going. It's THE place to be.
- Cinderella can't go to the ball. She does not have a gown. She has to stay home to clean the house.

Then we move into climax. The climax of the story is where the plot reaches its critical mass.

It's the tipping point where tensions are at their highest and the reader is most engaged by what's happening. The climax is usually where the most exciting or important actions occur.

- The Fairy Godmother shows up. Not only does she magically create the most beautiful gown for Cinderella, she also uses these magical spells to design slippers made of glass and turn her furry friends into a driver and footman. She turns a winter squash into the carriage and off Cinderella goes.
- Prince Charming sees only Cinderella in the sea of attendees. They dance, fall in love, and a future of abundance seems within reach.

The falling action occurs on the other side of the climax. Think of it like mountain climbing. Once you've reached the peak of the mountain, you have to come back down from the top.

Let's move into falling action. The clock strikes midnight. Oh, no, we all know the spells wear off at midnight. Cinderella better hurry or everyone in the town is going to see her disheveled dress and know that she's not who she appears. She runs out, leaving a shoe behind.

While the rising action helps build toward the climax, the falling action helps de-escalate the tension and ease readers into the conclusion of the story.

Last, but not least, the resolution of the story is where the plot comes to an end. This is where major problems are solved and loose ends are tied up.

- Prince Charming has the solution to the problem. Whoever fits this shoe is the woman he danced with at the Royal Ball and must be the woman he loves. And happily ever after is possible. The slipper fits!

WRITING AN EXCITING ARC

What is your story arc?

1. Exposition – Describe the character of your story and the details of the environment. Paint the picture for your audience.
2. Rising action – What's the challenge your character (big idea) is facing?

3. Climax – How did your big idea, story hit what seems to be the top? Identify the problem.

4. Falling action – What are you going to share with us that helps solve the problem?

5. Resolution – What are the learnings of your story? Share your big idea so that we can embrace this new way of thinking in our lives.

STORY ARC

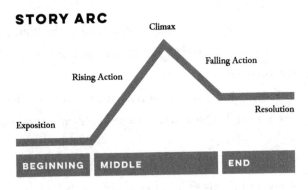

Exposition:

_____

_____

Rising action:

_____

_____

Climax:

_____

_____

Falling action:

_____

_____

Resolution:

_____

_____

RELATABILITY CAPTURES ATTENTION— HOLD ON TO IT

Part of being relatable when using your influential voice is being able to inspire someone instead of selling them, so they feel connected to you instead of separate from you. Having influence is not about convincing; it's about having the confidence and integrity to fully understand how to have the impact you desire to improve the lives of your audience. And the audience wants to feel connected to you and what you have to offer in your message.

Storytelling is innately human, so when someone appears to be immersed in your thought or emotion, you sense it. There is a reason that people walk out of my Speaker Salon showcases (www.speakersalonapplication.com), crying or laughing. It's not just because they fell in love with the presentation. They related in a personal way to the message. Most audiences are there because of you, so you already have the advantage of their time and attention. It's your responsibility to use that time and attention responsibly and wisely.

People make the same mistake over and over again whether they are heading up a boardroom, speaking from a big stage, or at the beginning stages of identifying their big idea. They either give the same talk and with the same delivery they've given for years, and their point of view has become totally unimpassioned and stale, no longer relating to the present moment. Or they try to sell their idea hidden in what they perceive to be their message, instead of inspiring. Both of these mistakes will prevent you from being relatable. And when that happens, your incredible message will not be heard. Let's look at how you can rely on being relatable by inspiring instead of selling your big idea.

Creating Relatability – 4 Ways You Can Rely on Being Relatable

1. Take "I" out of the equation.
2. Determine the problem.
3. Solve the problem.
4. Share its importance from your point of view.

1. Take "I" out of the equation.

Let's say you love talking about how to help people organize their homes and offices. You're passionate about decluttering their spaces, which you know will in turn declutter their minds, leading to emotional freedom.

Selling an idea:

- *I've been helping people organize their stuff for over ten years. I have seen what it does when I come in and help them let go of their things. It not only makes more room in their closet; it makes room in their soul. I have seen their transformation firsthand. This change must happen in order to live the fullest life and I can make it happen.*

Inspiring an idea we can embrace:

- *Stuff is matter, material, articles, and also the action of filling. Filling your home with matter, material in excess, might create an immediate feeling of safety and comfort. It can feel good to be surrounded by things. But it can feel great to be freed from your stuff and, ultimately, your need to hide. Clearing a path in your space will clear a path in your heart, leading to greatness, and it can start with just one room.*

- The word "I" was not used once here. The idea was gifted and relatable, while also offering a new way of thinking about it. You have inspired me to embrace the idea that I can organize my apartment. By starting small with just one room, I can become free and stop hiding.

2. Determine the problem.

You are a speaker who predominantly talks with women groups. And you desire to share that many women are not giving themselves permission to ask for what they want at home and at work.

Selling the idea:

- *Many women feel unworthy. I know it's difficult to give yourself permission to ask for what you are worth. I have seen this problem over and over in my work.*

Inspiring an idea we can embrace:

- *Asking for permission can be deeply connected to the darkest fears we all succumb to. But keep in mind that "I want" are two words that can change your life.*

- By sharing that you understand a problem and creating inclusivity by using "we," you are inspiring connection. Being relatable means your audience feels connected to you as a speaker. You've created a trust that you understand what the audience's fears are and illuminated that those fears can be tackled with the use of two little words. And because of this, I'm inspired to ask for what I want.

3. Solve the problem.

You are a web designer who speaks to entrepreneurs on the topic of building their business fast by using their website for marketing.

Selling the idea:

- *Building a list can take time, but with my design and SEO expertise, I'll teach you how to create a website for you that not only converts, but also stands out among the many similar websites in your field.*

Inspiring an idea we can embrace:

- *Website design is not limited to code and conversion. In addition to the solid content, images, and keywords, your brand and you will need to be represented in a way that will make you stand out from the rest. Your website is the digital home for your brand that your clients want to visit. Creating this home instills trust and ultimately faster expansion. And this is what you want in such an active marketplace.*

- This solves the problem of building a business fast by including the points of conversion and brand but also hitting on the personal connection, the marketplace and how you will stand out, which inspires us to embrace your idea.

4. Share its importance from your point of view.

You are a speaker who is giving a talk about the importance of community to entrepreneurs who desire to use the membership business model in their companies.

Selling the idea:

- *By creating a membership group, not only do you give your members access to a community and their businesses, but you also give them ongoing support in the Facebook group and the ability to give and receive feedback whenever they need it. It's money well invested on your part and the part of the community.*

Inspiring an idea we can embrace:

- *A membership community, this kind of unique group designed by you, not only supports one another by showing up to events and connecting personally and cheering one another on in your Facebook group, but also cultivates in your company a safe place to give and receive feedback, helping members thrive and improve by preventing the same mistakes. Nothing can be more valuable than learning what not to do in a safe and supportive membership community.*

- This is a very clear point of view. It's personal and specific. We get a clear understanding of what the membership community offers and that the business owner who starts a community needs to care about their group and desires to offer a safe and supportive place to connect. It's an inspiring introduction to a membership site that the business owners in the audience are inspired to embrace.

The impact of your message can ultimately reach anyone and everyone if your message is always inspiring and you strive to show us how you relate to us on a much deeper level. You open up your world and your voice to endless possibilities.

You inspire, which can solve the problems of people you are not even directly working with. That's global impact. You've just increased the number of people you serve without even knowing it. All because you've put your message out there and asked for nothing in return.

You don't have to sell us ideas. You just have to inspire us to embrace your big idea with authenticity. And this is what leads to relatability. Leadership giant John Maxwell says: "Being relatable as a leader doesn't mean being everyone's best friend. It doesn't mean saying or doing things that effectively bribe others into liking you. Being relatable means being yourself; living an authentic, consistent life with the people you lead. If you want better relationships, you must be relatable. It all begins with you—but it never ends there. Relating well with others creates a ripple effect that changes lives for the better."

And are you a leader as an influential voice? Without a doubt. Let's go deeper by answering these questions.

WRITING ON BEING A RELATABLE YOU

How are you being relatable when you are using your powerful voice for influence?

_____

_____

_____

How do you inspire your audience to embrace your idea?

_____

_____

_____

VULNERABILITY IS TRUE VICTORY

We are all praising the decision to embrace our vulnerability. Thank you to our hero, Brené Brown. In her riveting TED talk on the _Power of Vulnerability_, she illustrates that being vulnerable means sharing the most important, authentic parts of yourself with someone who matters to you—and risking rejection. Being vulnerable means being seen for who and what you are and exposing yourself to the potential for hurt. Although this may sound intimidating, the alternative is often worse. Being closed off can lead to loneliness and feeling unseen and unknown by others.

Also, I must add that Ms. Brown has a cameo in *Wine Country*, one of my favorite movies featuring Maya Rudolph, Amy Poehler, Tina Fey (I'm not asking for your feedback here; more on that in Chapter 5), and wow, do I wish I had been on that set when they shot it. Those are four of the most influential voices in Hollywood I know. And they also make me laugh more than anyone while I'm dancing to Wilson Phillips.

Vulnerability is something that you also have a responsibility to use wisely in your talks. If you are choosing to share a vulnerable story, a very personal story with us from a stage or from across the table, it's important to be clear on whether that story, oftentimes a personal trauma or tragedy, is ready to be told. If you have not healed from your experience, and truly healed, meaning tears are not streaming down your face during the delivery, it is too soon to use your voice in this way. It is your job to take care of the audience when you are on the big stage, and if we have to take care of you, you are not ready to share that story.

In 2018, Sarah Montana, writer for Hallmark Channel, a then-unknown speaker, sent in her written application for TEDx-LincolnSquare. Her speech was to be about forgiveness. She wrote about how her mother and brother had been murdered on Christmas Eve by someone they knew in the neighborhood. She went on to share that she knew forgiveness was important, and that she was able to do this, and by going on her journey from dark to light, she wanted to share with a wider audience how to forgive.

I was not going to ask her to move on to the next round, the video submission, based on her written application. I thought,

How can I listen to her speak and share this story and not feel sorry for her? And not feel bad as she shares this devastating idea? How is the audience going to be able to hear this talk? It's just too much.

At that moment, I knew I had to challenge myself to help this woman examine her own level of vulnerability so perhaps there would be a way to put her on the stage. Forgiveness is something that touches everyone in some way. Who wouldn't benefit from hearing her story? I had to give Sarah the opportunity to send a video submission about the idea of why forgiveness is important and *how* to actually forgive. She received this challenge with an open heart and open mind. To this day, Sarah's video submission is the most compelling I have ever received.

By sharing her story, Sarah has been healed and gives others the opportunity to also heal. And her TEDxLincolnSquare talk is now on the main platform at TED.com. That is pretty special! She is making a massive global impact. Sharing your impactful story will make a difference. By reaching just one person, you can change a life.

Being vulnerable does not mean sharing a traumatic experience to shock the audience. Being vulnerable means you are willing to share personal stories of shame, trauma, or tragedy with the desire to help others heal from theirs. It is imperative that you know whether you have healed.

When revealing a vulnerable truth, state it as fact. Do not embellish with emotion. Do not comment on what you've just said. For example, "I know, right?" Do not deflect and laugh it off as nothing; give the audience a beat to process before you move on.

Also, if you cry on stage during an emotional moment, you rob the audience of their potential tears. Use your voice to speak the truth and share the emotional moment, and give the audience the space to have the emotions for the first time. You've already experienced them in all their scary, cleansing, wonderful richness.

PROOF OF INFLUENTIAL SPEECH: TESTIMONIES

The U.S. Women's soccer team won its fourth World Cup on July 7, 2019, in France.

According to the *New York Times*, July 9, 2019, FIFA (Fédération International de Football Association) doubled the prize money for this Women's World Cup to $30 million and plans to double it again next time. Sounds too good to be true, doesn't it? It's actually a good ole slap in the face to gender parity. FIFA's contribution to the thirty-two men's World Cup teams is $400 million.

Gender discrimination has never been more in our faces, and unless all women demand equal pay, it means we are agreeing to being less than a man—in value and in worth.

In 1993, living in New York City and pursuing my dream of being a dancer, I joined the Doris Humphrey Repertory Dance Theater. I went to college for dance, and Doris Humphrey was a modern dance great who is part of the second generation of groundbreaking female modern dancers, including Martha Graham and Hanya Holm. Ruth St. Denis, Katherine Dunham, and Isadora Duncan are first generation. All these women are the pioneers who ushered in a new form of dance that protested traditional ballet.

They danced barefoot and without tights. This was revolutionary and truly influential.

Being able to bring Ms. Humphrey's choreography to life was an incredible gift for any dancer, and being paid to do it was unheard of. I was making $300 a week and loving every second of it. I got to play the lead in her *Two Ecstatic Themes*, choreographed in 1931, and *Lament for Ignacio Sanchez*, which she choreographed in 1946. This was historical and important to my career and my soul. My best friend was also in the company. We took ballet together before rehearsal. We danced together in rehearsal, and we roomed together when the company went on tour. This was a dream come true for a girl from Missouri who grew up on a farm. On tour in Salt Lake City, my best friend and I got back from rehearsal and we were unwinding in our shared hotel room. It was Friday, so we had just been given our paychecks for the week. Direct deposit wasn't a thing yet. We compared our paychecks in celebration that we were being paid to do what we loved. It was a naïve and benign moment of jubilation. Until I realized that my best friend, Andre, was being paid more than me. He was being paid more than me and, as the soloist, I was dancing more than him. This had to be a mistake. Gender discrimination? I was in New York City in a dance company. *No, this is an accounting error.* I didn't want to believe the numbers. I just couldn't! All seemingly rational thoughts. Well, when I confronted the artistic director, he informed me that he would "not increase my salary to equal Andre's, because it's more difficult to find male dancers than women." Blatant discrimination.

So, I quit. I quit being a soloist in a dance company in New York City, my dream.

Then, a week later, the artistic director served me with papers that said he was suing me for breach of contract. Being sued is a scary notion for anyone, but I was a dancer, which meant I didn't have a huge bank account. What did he think he would get out of me? A leotard? I marched straight down to Volunteer Lawyers for the Arts and put together a countersuit for discrimination. Needless to say, he went away. And I went on to dance with many more companies...and you know the rest. I had to speak up for the injustice being done to me and other female dancers. I didn't have to know their stories. They existed. If I had not turned my anger into something meaningful—and reclaimed my power—I realize now, as an influential voice, silence in a time that I needed to speak out may have caught up with me later in damaging ways.

Megan Rapinoe, star of the U.S. Soccer Team, led the 2019 tournament in goals and speaks openly about inclusion, gay rights, and equal pay. She joined her teammates in filing a federal lawsuit against U.S. Soccer to demand equal pay and treatment, a suit that Federal Judge R. Gary Klausner dismissed on May 1, 2020. When confronted at a press conference about her comments about not wanting to visit the White House, she stood by her statement before taking questions about the sport. She is role modeling for young women and men everywhere. She is not willing to accept being paid less and is risking public scrutiny by speaking out. She is using her platform responsibly to speak out, as she did on Twitter over the May 1 ruling. "We will never stop fighting for EQUALITY."

The Equal Rights Amendment, an amendment to the Constitution that was introduced by Alice Paul in 1923 and passed on to Congress in 1972, was designed to guarantee equal legal rights for all American citizens regardless of sex. It seeks to end the legal distinctions between men and women in terms of divorce, property, employment, and other matters. I'm proud to say that New York, along with eighteen other states, ratified ERA in 1972. Ratification has been staggered throughout the past forty-eight years. And Missouri, the state I'm from? Well, it has not ratified the amendment, so any young girl growing up in that state is being told she's not worth the same as the boys she shares a classroom with.

The more women fully wear our success, the more we own our power and be the leaders, the more we become speakers who understand that using our voice is our responsibility, the more we make change possible and probable.

Words have an incredible power to create hope and healing. In fact, Harvey Milk, the first openly gay elected official in the state of California, deemed his historical speech about unity and shattering stereotypes "The Hope Speech." It is still recognized for its story arc of hope, and he delivered that speech 1978.

Simultaneously, we know that words can demoralize and destroy. Coming from a world leader, words can start wars, ignite financial panics, and carry a nation through a troubled time. I will point you to a January 9, 2020, headline in *Forbes*: "Twitter Has Changed How World Leaders Can Communicate and May Have Stopped a War." Profound? To say the least! Timely?

Without a doubt. We've gone from sensationalized news and war propaganda in the newspapers of the 1800s needing to be picked up by individual hands to actually see the message, to a simple tweet (or 140 characters) that can be seen worldwide and ignite a firestorm in an instant.

A *USA Today* analysis of sixty-four rallies that U.S. President Donald J. Trump has held since 2017 found that, when discussing immigration, the president has said "invasion" at least nineteen times. He has used the word "animal" thirty-four times and the word "killer" nearly thirty-six times.

In addition, according to the database website Factbase, Trump used the expression "Chinese virus" more than twenty times between March 16 and March 30, 2020. The wording wasn't just a mishap or a careless joke. A photographer actually captured the script of a speech wherein Trump had crossed out the word "Corona" and replaced it with "Chinese."

These words of xenophobia, extremism, fear, and hate are being spoken from the highest office of our country. It is the kind of speech that wounds humanity on a level that will take decades to heal. If you think about our journey together to make you *The Influential Voice*, you fully understand what I am talking about here. Impact!

But this is not about sides. This is not about laws. This is about honoring and respecting the power of speech and bringing dignity back to soulful communication. Choosing to use the word "invasion" has consequences. Choosing to stay silent also has consequences. This is another reason your voice matters.

As communicators, it is crucial for us to think about how we are showing up in the world. As communicators, it is crucial to think about the power our words have and the weight they carry. It is also crucial to understand how staying silent can be equally as destructive.

On December 1, 2018, on the subway home from seeing Michelle Obama speak at Barclays Center in Brooklyn, I witnessed a group of young white boys talking with one another. It was around 10:00 p.m. and the train was moderately full of people. These five boys were speaking at a volume meant to be heard. And they were talking about two girls they went to school with. What was so shocking is they were talking derogatorily about these girls as if they were sexual property. They were speaking violence against two young girls in such a way that it became violence against all the women on the train, including me.

I stood up, walked over to these boys, and asked them to stop. (It was a crowded train; I was not in danger and I spoke to them, not to the entire train.) I shared that what they were saying was violent, and these young women needed to be respected with their language and actions. Of course, they were sarcastic with me, but they stopped. They laughed at me, but they stopped. They stopped speaking.

Had I been silent, they would have continued offending everyone on the train with their violent speech. My hope is that next time, the one boy in that group who knows this is wrong will have the courage not to remain silent. He, in turn, can help shape the others' behaviors moving forward. This is how we change the story of respectful communication.

We lost the great Toni Morrison, "Towering Novelist of the Black Experience," as the *New York Times* deemed her, in 2019. In 1993, she gave an acceptance speech for winning the Nobel Prize. "Fiction has never been entertainment for me. It has been the work I have done for most of my adult life. I believe that one of the principal ways in which we acquire, hold, and digest information is via narrative. So, I hope you will understand when the remarks I make begin with what I believe to be the first sentence of our childhood. That we all remember the phrase, 'Once upon a time.'"

We are in a moment in history where words are more important than ever. As communicators, as influential voices, we have an opportunity and a responsibility to rethink how we speak. As a people, we have an opportunity to create a new narrative, one that is driven by thoughtful and respectful speech.

I'm not asking for everyone to share in the same beliefs or have the same opinions. Our differences create endless possibilities governed by empathy, innovation, creativity, culture, and worldliness. However, speaking mindfully and deliberately from a place of love and respect is the only way we can change the current narrative or undignified communication.

Once upon a time... Let's write a new story. It's up to us.

10 RULES OF READINESS

- Think about what you are saying before you say it.
- Think about why you are saying it before you say it.
- Think about the consequences your words might have.

- When you make a mistake, acknowledge it.
- Take all the time you need to formulate your thoughts; we will wait.
- Spend time with people who know more than you and voraciously learn.
- Be willing to not know what to say and express that exactly.
- Increase your conscious awareness by practicing empathy in your speech.
- Own your place in the world and how you show up speaking.
- Get curious. Tell me more, instead of, "I don't know what you mean."

Influential Voice Imprints

Being an influential voice means being credible, vulnerable, and relatable.

Being an influential voice requires you to heal from trauma before you share it to serve others.

Being an influential voice calls on you to move from sell to inspire.

Being an influential voice means choosing to move beyond being good to being great by eliminating the "um," "so," and "you know" from your vocabulary.

Chapter 4

Fear and How It's Getting in Your Way: Guess What? It's Not about You

"According to most studies, people's number-one fear is public speaking. Number two is death. Death is number two. Does that sound right? This means to the average person, if you go to a funeral, you're better off in the casket than doing the eulogy."
—*Jerry Seinfeld*

KEY LESSONS

- You can coexist with fear and be influential on stage and off.
- Hormones activate a state of readiness when you rehearse with mild stress.
- Being in action creates instantaneous confidence.

- When you see and feel your performance, the stage becomes your playground.
- Comparing yourself to others is a habit you can and will break.

There are so many talks about fear. And there are so many people speaking on neuroplasticity and how you can rewire your brain out of fear. The reality is that fear is a big deal. When I googled fear, 133,000,000 results came up. Clearly, people are obsessed with fear. And various types of fear prevent countless human beings from doing phenomenal things that represent the beauty and zest of living.

For example, fear of rejection, fear of inadequacy, fear of uncertainty, and fear of failure are the top contenders of our psychological makeup that inhibit us from trying, flying, thriving. Have you stopped to unpack what fear really is? It's in your mind and not based on tangible or practical evidence in the here and now. Although sometimes it is legitimately based on the prospect of a negative repeat outcome (like I shouldn't run for the subway because of spraining my ankle right before a dance audition!), fear masquerades as fact. Fear is as real as any emotion, but you can learn to have a different relationship with it. This is also how you get over phobias, which are merely versions of fear on steroids. Face what you fear over and over again until its place within you and your potential becomes downsized rather than supersized.

Glossophobia, or a fear of public speaking, is a very common phobia and one that is believed to affect up to 75 percent of the population. YouGov presented more than two thousand people in the UK with an unlucky thirteen common phobias, asking them to rate their fear of each from "not at all" to "very afraid." Glossophobia rated third, after the fear of snakes and heights.

The underlying fear is judgment or negative evaluation by others, whether by a formal audience or within a group, on the spot.

We were all taught in Speech 101 or communication classes that effective communication skills boost confidence and self-esteem; increase influence, expertise, and connection; and can inspire new ways of thinking and elevate a cause. But you and I are here because delivering a powerful message can indeed change the world. It's obvious that without sharp communication skills, personal and professional attributes and abilities may be watered down or passed over, stunting progress and potential growth. At the same time, the inability to speak in public closes the door to precious resources for influencing decisions and motivating change. And the greatest change agents of all time are not necessarily politicians and CEOs; they are inclusion and diversity experts, entrepreneurs, advocates, parents, psychologists, and survivors. Every day, extraordinary people like you are daring to speak about the impact of self-imposed glass ceilings, creating community, resiliency, climate change, the practice of kindness, immigration, discrimination, and mental health...the list goes on.

Yes, fear can prevent you from taking a big stage. It can cause you to compare yourself to other speakers, as well as prevent you from applying to an event for fear of hearing no. But identifying what you fear is an important component to becoming an influential voice. Becoming intimate with your fear is paramount. Once you do, you can begin to manage and redirect your fear for good.

A healthy relationship with fear is a good thing. As counter-intuitive as it may seem at first, embracing fear about writing a big talk, using your voice, and taking a big stage is *exactly* the emotion that will propel you to the next level. If you do things you are afraid of, you are moving into consciousness and beyond limiting beliefs. We must do things we are afraid of if we want to have an influential voice. We must also do things we are afraid of without knowing what the outcome is going to be. I'm not suggesting you do things that are dangerous. I'm suggesting that you identify something that feels like fear and decide if this is a truth or a lie. Remember, if I had stayed in that apartment and not listened to the voice telling me to move because I was afraid of the "how" of finding a new apartment and the "what-if" I can't pay the rent (lie), I would not have written this book for you (truth).

I have been on thousands of stages in my career as a performer. And believe it or not, I had a lot of fear and nerves before going on. I would say to myself backstage, "Why am I putting myself through this? I'm freaking out. How can I go on?" Heart racing, palms sweating, nausea, anxiety. "What if...I fall, I faint, I mess up, I forget the steps and freeze, or what if I die?" These are the questions we all ask ourselves when it comes to sharing our important message from a big stage. Or even a boardroom.

I outgrew that kind of intense fear because of the repetition of the opposite experience. I never died, I never fainted, I rarely messed up. When I fell, I got back up, and when I forgot, I kept going. Yes, I have literally fallen down on stage during a show. And here I am, sharing it with you, to prove that you can get up and keep going. This is how you move beyond fear and into command of your audience on stage and off.

When you struggle with fear of performing, there are four things to remember that will help alleviate this kind of fear so that you can step into your purpose with confidence and connect with that person who's in need of your message.

- It's not about you.
- You must rehearse your speech under mild stress.
- Do something.
- Visualization helps.

1. It's not about you. It's about the audience and your idea.

"I'm so nervous. I hope I don't forget. I hope they like me." These "I" statements are exactly the fuel you do not want to add to the fire that is your nerves. When your focus is on you and how you feel, of course you're going to be and stay nervous. However, when you reframe the experience to be about the audience and the fact that you are sharing your gift with them so that they can walk away changed, then it's about them and your idea and there is nothing, nobody, nowhere that can keep you off that stage, no matter how profound your stage fright might be. Remember, you are meant to share your very important message, using your unique voice to change and even save someone's life.

One of my speakers whom I mentioned earlier (a vegan and lover of animals) suffers from profound stage fright. He is extremely shy and a classic introvert. Not that all introverts suffer from stage fright. When he got on stage at the Speaker Salon (www.speakersalonapplication.com), an incubator for speakers that I curate in New York City, he would grimace and shake. We as an audience felt the deep need to take care of him because he was so scared. There were two things I did to support him in moving through his fear. First, I reminded him that his idea of sharing the journey to a more compassionate life by becoming conscious of animals in our food, on our bodies, and in our zoos was an incredibly important idea to share with the world. Secondly, I reminded him that he needed to be the voice of those animals. Chickens can't tell the audience what happens in the factory farms. Minks can't share their experience of becoming a stole, and tigers are not able to express for themselves how it feels to be held captive and suffer from zoochosis.

Making it about the idea and the audience is how this speaker moved past intense fear and into a place of compassionate storytelling so he could elevate audiences to a more enlightened place of being in the world.

> *Ask Yourself:*
>
> **How can you ensure your talk is not about you?**
>
> **How can you be certain your talk is in service of the audience?**
>
> I know how important it is to share your voice with the world. I'm proud of you for acknowledging your fear and using it to level up.

2. Rehearse under mild stress, then increase that stress.

The reality is that your body is going to physiologically betray you when you get in front of people to speak. The stress hormones, adrenaline and cortisol, kick in and give you the gift of a queasy stomach, sweaty palms, shaking knees, and even shallow breathing. Yes, I do mean a gift! These hormones, though they're acting in accordance with fight-or-flight mode, will put you in a state of readiness that is going to elevate your speaking to another level. What's important here is that you start the process well in advance of your first speaking gig.

Rehearsing under mild stress, for example, in front of your roommate, partner, or spouse is a safe place to begin. This moment causes your body to experience a slight elevation of stress in the body but not enough to propel you into hysteria. Then increase that stress by delivering your talk in front of your colleagues at work. You increase the stakes slightly, hoping to do well but also knowing they won't fire you for being nervous. Then increase the stress even more, increasing the stakes and causing you to game up. Invite other speakers to be in your audience. Now, you are in an elevated state of fear and stress while still knowing consciously that it's not the actual speaking event, so you get to practice with nerves and you've forced yourself into a position of physiological distress in a safe environment. This proves to you and your subconscious that you *can* and *will* be able to deliver your talk while your body is physiologically betraying you. You will have rehearsed what it feels like to be nervous and get through it. You create a feedback loop that gives you the confidence to trust that being nervous, being afraid, and living to see another day is possible.

When you do rehearse under mild stress in front of folks, be certain to put feedback boundaries in place. (We'll cover this a little later.)

3. Do something, literally anything.

When an actor is playing a scene and it's not landing, or they are clearly in their heads and not showing up authentically, I give them something to do. Let's say one of my actors has in their head the idea of how the scene should play out, how they should feel, and how they are supposed to be "acting." This is the exact opposite of what they need to be experiencing. Being in the moment, right or wrong, is how we are going to drop into the truth of a scene and play it in a way that connects to an audience or a scene partner.

You've seen it before—you are watching a play or speaker and you are not connecting. You may not know why but you aren't. You feel too still or stagnant, with a sensation of awkward space or distance. It's usually because the actor or the speaker is fearful of being intimate or vulnerable, or they are afraid of relinquishing control and they block us from experiencing the truth of the moment. Actors direct the scene instead of playing it. The speaker imposes themself onto you instead of allowing you to receive the idea from them. When I see this in a rehearsal room, I give the actor something to do. "Here's a deck of cards; I'd love for you to play that scene again while playing gin rummy."

Now, if the scene is not in support of this artistic action, I would give them something else to do, like washing the dishes. By giving the actor something to do, I ensure that they are now forced in the moment. They can't manufacture how they are experiencing the scene because they are doing something while saying the lines. The same thing happens on stage for a speaker.

My vegan speaker, who was finally moving past stage fright by speaking for the animals and understanding the importance of why the audience needed to hear his big talk, was beginning to deliver the performance the same way. It was becoming mundane and monotonous. At a rehearsal, I went on stage with him, grabbed anything I could find (stools, brooms, mops, music stands, chairs, extension cords), and dumped it all onto the stage. Needless to say, he was looking at me like I was crazy and so were the other speakers in the Speaker Salon. I asked him to clean up the stage, putting everything back in its proper place, while he delivered his talk. He was doing something; he had a goal that replaced performing, so he stopped thinking about "performing" his talk.

The stage was clean! Most importantly, his talk was fantastic and stirring...finally.

4. Visualization and actualization help.

Being on stage alone is scary; whether you're a dancer, an actor, or a public speaker, all eyes are on you. There is nowhere to hide. And perhaps that is why a friend who studied acting in college still, twenty-five years later, dreams of being on stage in front of an audience and not being able to deliver her first lines because she forgot them or is just too nervous to open her mouth. She can't hide and she is absolutely tongue-tied while all eyes are on her. And yet, she still walks onto that stage. Because she visualizes everything going right. She sees the perfect scene playing out. She feels it in her body. When you see the stage in your mind and feel the energy of the audience ahead of time, you are setting yourself up for success. When you see yourself delivering your talk with power and grace, you will deliver your talk with power and grace. When you allow your body to feel the emotion of confidence and effortless delivery, you can re-create this on the day you take the stage. When you allow yourself to feel the emotions of receiving a standing ovation, you will set yourself up to deliver a standing-ovation-worthy talk. See it. Feel it. Trust it. It is yours. You are an influential voice.

Some of us may feel prepared, of course. Although we might be mentally prepared and emotionally ready, our bodies are going to betray us. Like I said, there will be a physiological response. There's no way to control all of our body's responses, but we can certainly manage them. Here is a practice to help order your fear right before you go on stage:

Plant both feet on the floor, feel how solid the ground is that you are standing on and allow that to transfer up through your legs and into your body. You are standing strongly and solidly. Nothing can knock you over. Connect to the earth. Breathe deeply. Ground your energy. When you inhale slowly in through your nose and out through your mouth, you'll slow down your heart rate and calm yourself. And trust. Just like Michael Jordan, who stood at the free throw line for hours to prepare. Trust the work you've done. You're ready.

SUREFIRE TIPS

- *Say the first line of your talk before you go out.* This will not only ground you; it will also ensure you will be on point for the entire talk. Knowing you nailed that first line puts the audience in the palm of your hand and gives you the confidence you need.

- *Begin when you are ready.* So many speakers take the stage and begin talking before they are ready. They feel hurried to start because everyone is staring at them. They begin before they are ready and then we can feel that frenetic energy for the next ten minutes, which is how long it's going to take for you to win us back and calm us down. Ground yourself and then begin. We will wait.

- *Accept the gift of the audience before you give them yours.* The audience is giving you their time and energy, so receive that before you give them the gift of your talk. The third tip will also support the first and second. When you say that first line, accept the gift from the audience before you give them yours, *and* begin talking only when you are ready, you are going to become far more masterful at the art of public speaking.

FEAR OF COMPARISON TO OTHERS IS A QUITE FRIGHTFUL BAD HABIT

Fear is not limited to stage fright. I have seen speakers get into a cycle of ego, fear, and comparison with other speakers. Ultimately, this combination is devastating. When you live in the trifecta of ego, fear, and comparing yourself to others, you are not only hurting yourself, caught up in the illusions of self-doubt and self-deprecation, you are also slowing down the process of your being amazing and having an influential voice.

I bring this to your attention because as a director, one of my jobs is to observe. I watch and wait. I have to be patient with my actors because they are also in process. I can't expect perfection out of the gate. In addition to waiting, I also observe their insecurities, their behaviors, and their achievements. I watch them. It's my job. I may not love something they are doing, but I wait because they may organically stop. Or not, and that's when I decide to ask them to change it. It's the process.

I get a lot of questions in the process, in the room, like, "Do you want me to cross on this line? Do you want me to play this with more anger or sadness? Is this reading?" Purposefully, I often answer, "I'm not sure yet." This is because sometimes, I'm really not sure yet! Other times, I want them to find it on their own because they know the characters more than I. They are inside the characters!

Once I've waited for a while, if they are still stuck or need my support, I'll direct. I'll tell the actors what I want them to do and they do it. This process I describe is exactly the same with my speakers. The other thing that is exactly the same is that when a speaker or an actor allows ego, fear, and comparison to sneak into their worlds, everything begins to unravel. You cannot do your best work when you are making it about you.

This trifecta not only keeps you stuck; it makes you crazy, frustrated, and annoyed because you are no longer on your own path. When you veer onto someone else's path, you absolutely cannot do the work you are meant to be doing. You cannot play two characters at once. You cannot be two speakers at once. As author, spiritual leader, politician, and activist Marianne Williamson says: "Our deepest fear is not that we are inadequate. Our deepest fear is that we are powerful beyond measure. It is our light not our darkness that frightens us. We ask ourselves, who am I to be brilliant, gorgeous, talented and fabulous? Actually, who are you not to be?"

So, who are you *not* to be? When you feel your ego step in and compare yourself to another speaker, stop. When you fear that another speaker is talking about your topic, stop. When you feel the ego take over, stop. This is a decision you can make. So make it.

Be the speaker you are meant to be. Stay on your beautiful and unique path and trust the process. It's okay to not have all the answers yet. Simply play the scene until it all makes sense. Take this in as truth.

FEAR OF NOT BEING CHOSEN

When we don't get chosen, it's usually a gift. It usually means not yet.

When I am casting a show, a film, the Speaker Salon, or my event, The Big Talk Live, I have to say no to people. I have to pass.

Ask Yourself:

How are you going to identify a moment of ego?

This might look like when you find out that you are talking about something that your friend in the community is also talking about and all of a sudden you feel a moment of, "How could they? That's my idea." Remember what I said about POV? You can both talk about fear or the gut micro-biome and do it eloquently and uniquely.

How are you going to identify a moment of comparison?

This could look like when you say to yourself, "Wow, I'm never going to be able to perform like they did. They nailed it, so I might as well throw in the towel." Remember what I said about how not sharing your idea is being selfish? There will be no towel throwing here, please.

What are you going to do to set yourself up for success?

This goes back to trust and identifying the truth versus the lie. "My talk is not good enough." Lie. "I'm not special enough to share my important story." Lie. "Everyone else is an influential voice, not me." Lie.

Are you willing to do the work in writing your talk? Are you willing to do the work in rehearsing your talk? Are you the person to share a very important message, through your POV, so that you can change and even save a life? This is the truth. Hear me. This is the truth.

I have to choose someone else. These decisions are complex and multifaceted, and it's important to me to clarify what that means when I, or anyone else who has integrity, pass. And why this initial no is a gift.

Back when I was performing, I wanted everything right now. I wanted to be in Paul Taylor's Company dancing *Esplanade*, one of his three most famous pieces. I wanted to be doing the sizzling hot *Fosse* on Broadway. I wanted to be a Spice Girl, and yes, I auditioned for the American version of the group.

I wanted what I wanted because I was ready. And that's the lesson here: my declaration that I was ready. I mean, declaration is a pretty strong statement, right? Still, the Universe knew I was not ready. And that's the gift. The people who didn't cast me saved me from a lot of heartache and, frankly, the premature advancement of a potentially limited career. The successful career I have today is because people said no to me. I'm deeply grateful to all of you, the choreographers, theater producers, production companies, and directors who said no to me. Your gift has kept on giving, and I'm deeply humbled and filled with gratitude for you.

For example, had I been hired to dance at Taylor, I would have traveled the world dancing the most prolific and profound works of the American treasure that is Paul Taylor and his incredible body of work. However, because I was not cast, I was inspired to use my grit to think beyond that which I thought was the only thing I would ever do. I had to think about what more was possible. I did not walk through the door (on Broadway between Spring Street and Prince Street in the early '90s), so instead, I designed and constructed my own door. I began to build my own doors to walk through over and over. I would not have considered producing my own work, the way I want it to be produced, had I been on tour with Paul Taylor.

If I had gotten cast in *Fosse*, I would not have considered telling other people's stories because I would have been solely obsessed with Bob Fosse's provocative tales told via dance. He was a genius, winning a Tony, Oscar, and Emmy in the same year. If you have not seen *All That Jazz*, run to Amazon now. It's one of the most incredible works of art ever made.

The reason it's a gift to not be chosen is because this pushes you. The gift of no gives you an opportunity to prove us wrong and to come back fighting. Because trust me, no often means not yet, and could eventually mean yes.

When I was producing TEDxLincolnSquare, a speaker emailed me, "I'm writing to say that I would very much like to be considered for your upcoming TED event. I just got married and would like to talk about my wife." I somewhat sarcastically and somewhat endearingly thought, *Ah, that is adorable…and not an "idea worth spreading."*

I asked him to rethink his idea and pitch me again. This was a "not yet." He came back to me with another idea that was still not a yes. And he came back for a third time with the idea that landed him on my TEDx stage. Had he heard no the first time and allowed fear to stop him, he would not have gone on to be one of the most powerful talks about political polarization I've ever seen.

YOU ARE NOT ALONE

In all my years of producing different shows and events, the one thing that remains the same is that two weeks before the event or the show, fear sets in. This occurs no matter whether you are a seasoned speaker or a new one. No matter whether you have done one thousand shows or one. It is consistently about two weeks before that fear sets in because the speakers or actors are far enough out that they start imagining everything that can go wrong, but not too close to the performance that they begin to manifest the failures. These fears range from forgetting the lines to being rejected to feeling like they are not worthy.

I had the privilege of working with three top speakers on their TEDx talks during the same period of months, all taking stages on June 23, 2019. What I learn every time in this process is that it unfolds like this:

Each speaker starts out with excitement. Then we move into the process, which is not easy. It takes lots of time, thought, and more thought to write, listen to, rewrite, and deliver a talk. Then they move into the *insecurity* phase. "Is this any good? How am I going to edit my idea down to eighteen minutes? Who do I think I am to be talking about such a big idea?" From there, because of the work, we move into the *confidence* phase. "This talk is going to help so many people. I'm the absolute right person to be sharing this idea worth spreading. I am off book and ready to deliver a game-changing talk."

This next phase is the phase I welcome and, frankly, love. The fear phase is when the mind begins to take over. "What

if I forget everything? What if they reject me? What if I die?"
Alarm bells. *Panic!*

It is at this point that we take an inventory of everything we need to do to set up for success, so that on the day, there is no room for fear. So that on the day, all there is room for is delivering an incredible message and having impact on the audience and the world.

Just like an athlete seeing the ball going into the net, your mind is going to visualize your success from that stage. However, if you are thinking about what you need to do right before you go on, this kind of distraction can fuel the fear that will be in the way of your captivating performance. Free your mind from fear and worry so it can do what it's meant to do: be with the audience.

Reducing or even eliminating fear starts by removing any and all things that can go wrong. My speakers and I create a list of everything they need, of everything they want, and of everything that will ensure their success on the day. This level of preparation is what gives you the freedom to be fully in the moment on stage. And this is how you deliver a rock star performance every time. When you are about to go on stage, it's an opportunity to shine.

Here is a checklist for you to refer to so you can focus on being a captivating speaker, an influential voice:

Captivate and Influence Checklist
- *Get a good night's sleep.* Fly in the day before so you can get a sense of the space, get to know the audio-video team, and then get a good night's sleep. You never want to fly on the day of in case the flight is delayed, or you will be totally stressed out.

- *Drink tons of water.* When you are hydrated, your brain fires on all cylinders, your skin glows, and your mouth is lubricated to give an amazing talk.
- *Have slippery elm lozenges on hand.* If you do suffer from a dry mouth when nerves kick in, slippery elm lozenges will help you stay lubricated. Just pop one in before and then take it out right before you go on.
- *Make sure your clicker has new batteries.* Always use your clicker, as you know how it feels and you know which button advances. And you do not want it to stop working midtalk. Fresh batteries and an extra set on hand will always reduce the stress of the unknown.
- *Bring your PowerPoint on a second USB drive.* Always have a backup. You worked very hard on your slide deck, so never leave it to the Universe or an event organizer to have it. Even if you sent it ahead, travel with your USB drive and rest easy.
- *Run through your talk once really fast in the morning, without emotion.* When you do an "Italian" run, which is what it's called in theater (I'll explain why in Chapter 5), you flex the muscles and get the synapses firing without attaching emotion to the talk, so when you do deliver, it's fresh and sounds unrehearsed.
- *Make sure the shoes you are wearing allow you to feel grounded.* You do not want to be thinking about

how badly your feet hurt before you go on stage. Nobody cares about your stilettos. They care about your message and how you are going to deliver it.

- *Dress like you, not like someone you want to be.* Dress for the venue, but also like yourself. If you never wear dresses, don't start now. If you are not a suit guy, no need to put on a suit and feel uncomfortable. Be you.

- *Be sure to own who you are, not who you think people want you to be.* If you are not authentically you, the audience won't know why, but they won't be able to trust you. When you are yourself, people feel it and drop in with you.

- *Visualize yourself on that stage.* When you can see yourself on that stage succeeding, it creates a space for you to be captivating and simply focus on sharing your message.

WRITING ABOUT FEAR

How have you realized your potential today by acknowledging fear and how it can serve you?

_____

_____

_____

_____

What is your not yet? How are you going to turn it into yes?

_____

_____

Whom are you comparing yourself to and how are
you going to stop?

_____

_____

> *Influential Voice Imprints*
>
> An influential voice hears "no" as "not yet."
>
> An influential voice knows there's room
> for everyone's unique POV.
>
> An influential voice is always prepared, for anything
> and everything.
>
> An influential voice is willing to trust the
> truth and eliminate the lie.

Chapter 5

Rehearsal, Performance, and Feedback: A Total Technique Package

> "I prepare myself for rehearsals
> like I would for marriage."
> —*Maria Callas*

KEY LESSONS

- Repetition goes hand in hand with confidence.
- Pair memorization with a fun activity for the best result.
- When a space is safe, authentic, and intimate, decisions come much easier.
- Taking command of a stage requires attention to detail.
- Powerful speaking happens on stage and off.

BEING YOUR OWN COURAGEOUS COACH:
REHEARSAL

The definition of plié is a movement in which a dancer bends their knees and straightens them again, usually with the feet turned out and heels firmly planted on the ground. This is called "first position." I had an extensive dance career. I began at the age of seven and danced well into my forties. I've had both of my knees operated on, along with my foot. Being an athlete is a serious commitment. And I've done a million pliés.

Pliés are the foundation of any dancer, not just a ballet dancer. Every step we accomplish starts from, moves through, and ends with a plié, a bend and straightening of the legs. The plié is our preparation, our transition, and our landing. But nobody wants to watch a bunch of bends and straightens. They want to see a virtuosic grand jeté, or "big throw," into the air and multiple pirouettes landing on a dime, not the pliés that make this possible. In order for pliés to disappear so that the dance is revealed, however, we need to do pliés over and over again. And over and over again some more.

Repetition is everything when it comes to rehearsal. Rehearsal is your pliés or your biceps curls, for all you gym folks. Your talk needs to be revealed to the audience. We don't want to see how you are getting into it and how you're getting out of it. The blood, the behind-the-scenes view. It's not pretty or influential, and it doesn't have to be. It's the work. We do not want to watch you search for the words or stumble over the content. We simply want to be mesmerized and wowed by it, so that we are transported and transformed. We don't want to see your effort and don't want to see you fall off pointe. You have to rehearse. You need to know your talk forward, backward, and inside out.

Memorizing takes time. And trust me, you will believe you are memorized in the soul of your being, and the second you get in front of someone, the words will go out of your head. I have seen this happen to countless speakers. When I'm producing one of my shows, TEDxLincolnSquare or Speakers Who Dare or now, The Big Talk Live, and it's time for the speakers to run through their talk with me, they all start over because they get nervous and lose their words. I actually had a speaker do her entire talk in a rehearsal with her back to me because facing me caused her to have talk amnesia. Be sure to give yourself plenty of time to get off the book, which is knowing the talk without your script. Many speakers resist memorizing a script. They say it makes them feel inauthentic, not in the moment, stifled even.

I'd love you to consider if an actor took the stage and spoke these words:

"So, my friends and brothers who might believe in what I do. I know it's kind of hard and you might feel scared, but if you support this cause, many people will probably revere you afterwards. Trust me." Instead of what's actually written by William Shakespeare:

> *We few, we happy few, we band of brothers;*
> *For he to-day that sheds his blood with me*
> *Shall be my brother; be he ne'er so vile,*
> *This day shall gentle his condition:*
> *And gentlemen in England now a-bed*

Shall think themselves accursed they were not here,
And hold their manhoods cheap whiles any speaks
That fought with us upon Saint Crispin's day.

The Saint Crispin's Day speech from *Henry V* is one of the most incredible speeches ever written. When you begin to write your big talk and spend hours choosing each word, each combination of words for the kind of impact you desire, I promise that memorizing will become as important as your delivery. Your words are important and saying them the way you've written them honors you, your voice, and the process.

When you move past the threshold of thinking you know your talk and into the phase of the memorization where it becomes part of your DNA, then you are free to play and experience the freedom of knowing your talk so confidently and fully that you are in total command of the talk and the audience. Do your pliés. Do your biceps curls. They are totally boring, and you will want to stop. But don't, because what's on the other side of your rehearsal is absolute freedom.

Antesa Jensen, emotional intelligence expert and TEDx speaker, said this:

> In my work with Tricia leading up to my TED talk in Chicago, I bumped up against a lot of the process of memorization. Which was a really tricky area for me v I have a background in music and I really struggled with the process of practicing something so diligently that it gets into your bones. Something that I pride myself on is my authenticity and my

presence and I was really worried that the process of writing a script and then memorizing it and then delivering it on stage would ultimately take away from an audience's ability to feel me and my authentic self. Tricia assured me that there would come a point in the process where the script would be so heavily embedded in my DNA that my authenticity would come back and it would no longer sound like I was reading my script. And I gotta be honest, I didn't believe her. I really genuinely thought she was totally nuts and leading me astray. However, I trusted Tricia. I trusted Tricia's expertise. I trusted Tricia's process in this and kind of blindly let her lead me into a place I'd never been before. And we were inching up to my talk and I was really starting to panic that this wasn't going to happen. And all of a sudden it clicked. Everything was in my DNA, the bicep curls really paid off. I went on stage and nailed it, was totally authentic and was able to connect with my audience. I trusted Tricia, even though I didn't believe her at the time, to lead me into a process that I had never been to in my own growth and the result was really extraordinary. I'm so blown away by going through that process and having the moment on stage feel tremendously effortless. It was really something special.

IMPRINTS AND INFLUENCE: THE MEMORIZATION TECHNIQUE

First, start by memorizing each section of the talk that leads up to a beat change. A beat change is a new thought. When you have that section memorized and in your DNA, move on to the next section. Once that section is part of your cellular makeup, go back to the transition between the two sections. Now, rehearse that transition. That would be the sentence at the bottom of the first paragraph and the top of the next. Tie those two sentences together in your mind. Now, deliver both of the first two sections together. If you can do this without fumbling, you may move on.

Do this process until you've strung the entire talk together without any memory issues. If you are noticing that you continually flub it up in certain sections of the talk, go back to the writing. You have probably either written a sentence that is not how you speak, or you have written a sentence that is similar to another section and it's confusing your mind. Give yourself permission to rewrite it instead of being hard on yourself because you keep messing up in the same place. There is a good reason you are, and you can fix that. Keep in mind, too, this is not performance rehearsal. This is purely your pliés and biceps curls. Just get the words into your DNA. Performance comes later. And performances in the rehearsal room ahead of the event are called run-throughs. When you are doing a run-through, you are meant to stay in the moment, never breaking, no matter what. This is what makes a run-through different from a rehearsal. Rehearsals stop and start in order to make adjustments. They are not your performance of the work.

Do not mistake rehearsal alone for a run-through. Because if you do not actively do your run-throughs (performing the talk top to bottom, as if you are on stage, in front of your audience, without stopping and looking at your script) prior to taking the stage, you will make the mistake of showing an audience your rehearsal and not your performance.

The hit single "Sunglasses at Night" catapulted Canadian-born Corey Hart onto the charts overnight in 1983.

I remember driving in my red Sunbird with his first album, *First Offense*, blasting from the cassette player of the dashboard. Every day to and from school, I would have the volume cranked to ten as I sang along, knowing every word to every song. I was seriously obsessed with him. I went to see him live in concert and went on to buy his next two albums, *Boy in the Box* and *Fields of Fire*, neither of which kept him on the top of the charts. Nobody listened to these albums and they weren't played on the radio, but I still knew every single word to every single song.

I share this with you because we think memorization happens by standing in front of the mirror reciting your big talk or your toast or your keynote over and over. Yes, if you recited your talk over and over, you will eventually memorize it. However, I point out that the consistency and split focus of me listening to Corey Hart while driving to and from school for weeks is why I memorized all of his songs to perfection. I was not only rehearsing; I was doing two things at once, and I was having fun. When you are taking on the epic task of memorizing your big talk, find ways to make it fun while you are doing something else. Get out your water colors and paint a bouquet of flowers that you can share with your family after your rehearsal. Grab a basketball and hit the court. Nobody will care that you are talking to yourself. And if they do, invite them to be your impromptu audience as you play some one-on-one. Make a five-course meal for your friends and after rehearsal you'll be ready to feast! There are also mundane things you can do for memorization success. Do the dishes, do the laundry, drive. Record yourself giving the talk and listen to it everywhere you go. Listen to it when you are running on the treadmill or in the park. Listen to it when you are driving to and from work. Speak it along with yourself. Do your talk and if you forget one word, start over from the beginning.

Another technique to intensify and solidify your memorization process is to recite your talk as fast as possible. In theater, we refer to a really fast run-through of a show as an *Italian*. That term came from the Italian nineteenth-century opera companies that had a lightning-fast rehearsal process of running through words without acting. This also gets your synapses firing rapidly, so that you get feedback on the dots that are not connecting and can focus more on that section of the talk. When the talk comes pouring out of you at this emotionless, rapid-fire pace, you will literally train your mind to know what comes next. The talk pours out of you on that stage and you can focus on performance instead of searching for the words.

Memorizing will also continue in the rehearsal process, once you move into the performance phase of the process. Come into rehearsal *on book* (with your script) and as you begin to block the talk, you'll make notes in your script, when to walk where and why. This is your choreography. You want to rehearse your talk, not only so it sounds like you are talking to us, not reciting a perfectly memorized speech, but also so you know the blocking. The blocking of your talk not only helps you memorize, but also this choreography will add importance, humor, and impact to what you are saying.

Once your talk is memorized and blocked, do it on its feet over and over again. Know when you move, pause, stand still, and change focus and know why. If you walk downstage (toward an audience) the meaning of that may be so you connect deeply with them. It could also mean you want them to feel your energy in a more direct way. If you move upstage (away from the audience) by backing up, understand that this needs to be conscious. If you back away, it's because you want them to feel you disconnect or pull away for a reason. Maybe you want them to feel a certain way because of a section of your talk. If your objective is for them to feel separate, then physically separate. If you want them to feel potentially on the same level as you, literally walk off the stage and into the audience. If you want them to feel urgency from the top of your talk, run into the space. I spent years on stage not speaking, just moving. And I always had my audience in the palm of my hand. I knew how to transport them by choosing how to dynamically move and when to own them with stillness. I never said a word.

Once you feel like you know your talk and the choreography on its feet, then change it up entirely. Move to the seated position. Do your talk seated so you cannot rely on the movement to cue you. Remove one of the cues purposely so that you become intimately acquainted with the parts of the talk you do not know. Then move to rehearsing seated with your eyes closed. Removing another sense from the process forces you to really move past the threshold of knowing your talk into the place of it literally being in your DNA. When you forget one word, start over from the beginning. It's all about the repetition and changing up how you rehearse so that you are certain you know the talk no matter the outside circumstances.

PERFORMANCE ON PURPOSE: THE TECHNIQUES

When I'm in a room with a group of actors and we begin the rehearsal process, it's my job to create a safe space for everyone. If the space feels safe, then authentic and intimate decisions can be made. The actors trust that they can make bold choices, take risks, knowing this is a safe place to fail big. Failing is one of the most delicious things to experience in the rehearsal process, and this is how you get to a magnetic and captivating performance, by going through the process and not around it.

Be willing to be uncomfortable.
- If you withhold something in rehearsal because you are uncomfortable, you may prevent the perfect way of entering, opening, or even closing your powerful talk from being born.

Be willing to fail.
- Make a bold choice, like opening your talk in song and see if it works. If it doesn't, who cares. Nobody got hurt!

Be willing to make a bad decision.

- Maybe facing upstage during your talk is a bad decision, but if you don't try, you'll never know what a better decision might look like.

Now, you get to put into practice becoming conscious from Chapter 2 in relationship to your performance. The audience wants you to succeed. When you are the expert giving a talk, the audience is there for you. They want to hear what you have to say. They believe in you and your idea, which is why they are in the audience in the first place.

Become conscious about your performance.

Get clarity around what story you're telling. Telling your personal story creates vulnerability and relatability. Telling the story of someone else allows you to teach us through the lessons you learned and recount it for our benefit.

Determine whether you are telling a personal story or a story about a secondary character. We need to root for one leading role. Bouncing between your story and the story of another splits our focus and causes us to not care about either character. Or worse, we begin to compare them in our minds.

Then ask yourself what you want the audience to feel. When your audience feels something during your talk, they will never forget what you shared with them. It will be seared into their minds because their emotions were involved.

Determine which emotions you want the audience to experience during your talk and make sure your talk takes the audience on that ride. If you want the audience to feel safe,

embrace them by standing close to the downstage playing space. If you want them to feel uneasy, walk on stage and stand there for a while before you speak. If you want them to feel empowered, paint the picture of possibility for their own lives.

Show your heart. A cold speaker is a detached speaker. An influential voice is someone who's willing to be vulnerable, honest, and raw.

- When you let your guard down and expose yourself to the audience, we can relate to you, trust you, and like you. Human beings want to belong. We want to feel a part of something, and by sharing your truth and letting us in, you become the captivating human being, leader, and speaker we want to follow.

Speak an uncomfortable truth. Perfection is a waste of time. And it's dishonest. Nobody is perfect and if you keep trying to keep that façade going, you're once again preventing the connection with another person who needs you.

- When you share a personal story about yourself that reveals a failure or a struggle, the audience will root for you and feel connected to you. Failure is always an opportunity to teach the lessons you learned in service of others.

Body language matters. Being mindful of your gestures, your stance, and your overall physicality must always be considered.

- Nonverbal communications are oftentimes stronger than verbal ones. Think about what happened at the presidential debate between Hillary Clinton and

Donald Trump. He was totally silent when she was speaking, yet his stalking of her spoke for itself.

- If you are pacing and agitated, the audience will be agitated too. If you are calm and grounded, you will put the audience at ease so they can take in your very important words.

Dramatic gestures can support dramatic content. I'm a dancer. I also know the importance of when to be still and when to be dramatic. Know the difference and be memorable every time you take the stage.

- When you are saying something very important you may want to use physicality to emphasize the moment. Running to stage right to deliver an impactful thought could invoke a feeling of urgency for us. Entering with music and dancing into the space will evoke a lively experience for the audience. Raising your arms up to the sky during the climax of your talk could bring us home. Be sure, however, that you do not mistake using dramatic gestures that are authentic and those that are manufactured and cheesy.

Stillness is highly effective. Being still is hard and, when done well, extremely powerful.

- When you choose to be still, what you are saying lands on us hard. Stillness is a movement choice that has lots of impact. If I want my audience to lean in or look up from their notebook or phone, I will move into stillness. That does not mean I stop moving. It means I will walk to a location on the stage and wait. I take command of my stage and my audience. You can do this too. Moving into stillness is a powerful tool for being captivating.

Tone makes a difference. The world of texting has completely removed our ability to read tone. However, your influential voice on stage and off requires a clear mastery of tone.

- Your voice and facial expressions must align. If you do not believe what you are saying, neither will we. If you think what you are saying is worthwhile and important, so will we.

- If your voice is confident, yet your face is showing fear, the audience will not know why they can't trust you. The misalignment will create confusion, which leads to distrust. And this is when they stop listening. It's your responsibility to always make sure an audience hears every word you share. Your voice matters, and what you have to say is important.

Be aware of lilting upwards at the end of a sentence. "I'm so happy to be here" Period or question mark?

- When you end a sentence on an upward lilt, it immediately becomes a question. Do not question us throughout your talk. We want to know you are the expert by the statements you are making.

Smile and make eye contact. Look at the people you are talking to. Look right into their souls. You are sharing powerful and urgent information. These gifts are going to go in through their eyes and penetrate their hearts.

- When you smile and make eye contact with the audience, we see that you are in control of the situation and we stop worrying about you. You never want an audience to have to take care of you. When you look above us or past us or over our heads, we are not sure who you are talking to and we fear you may not care about us.

Start strong and finish impactful. Walk onto the stage in full command of the experience from start to finish. That means staying fully present and "in" the talk. It means not allowing any distractions to pull you "out" of the talk.

- Tell the audience what they can expect for the next forty-five minutes.
- Pique their curiosity by sharing that you're going to reveal something at the end that is going to blow their minds.
- Share something about which most people may not know, so the audience will want to stick around and hear your entire talk.
- Provide a shock factor. "I was homeless and I'm here to share my story."
- Share a story or a statistic that is shocking so the audience will be encouraged to stick around to

hear your solution. "Did you know that the average person waits six months of their life waiting for a red light to turn green?"

Speak with power and emphasis. You are the expert. You are the speaker on stage. That means you are in charge. Own the stage.

- End each sentence with clarity and certainty. Use volume to make an important word or thought stand out. Speak slowly or quickly to make a point in another way. Be direct, confident, and unapologetic.

- Drive the final point home with passion. Allow your emotions to shine through, taking the idea home, so we know how you feel and it will become contagious.

Plan the ending word for word.

Doris Humphrey, an American treasure whom I mentioned earlier, was a choreographer of the early twentieth century. She went on to have a massive impact on the culture of dance in this country. She also wrote a book called The Art of Making Dances, *which I studied in college. In it, she writes, "A good ending is 40 percent of the dance. The ending is a highly important affair, which choreographers should worry about fully as much as playwrights with their third act curtain. The theater is a place where the last impression is not only the strongest one, but trends to color the audience's opinion of the whole, which is perhaps not fair, but it's a fact."*

You want to be rock solid on how you end your talk. If you memorize anything, it must be the ending, so that you can ensure you nail it and leave the lasting impression you desire.

WHAT YOU WANT MATTERS: OBJECTIVE AND ACTION

Think about your objective. Finish this sentence: I want the audience to...

Objective and Action is the technique I use with my actors and my speakers. This technique is something we as human beings unknowingly rely on in our everyday lives. For example, if you want your spouse to take out the trash, that's your objective. How you get them to do that is your action.

Performance Technique Used On Stage and Off

Objective: I want someone to cross the street. Action: How I get them to do it.

- I invite them. ("I'd love for you to walk on the shady side of the street with me; I'm not wearing any sunscreen today.")
- I beg them. ("Please cross the street; I'd really love for us to walk by these store windows together.")

- I scare them. ("I saw someone over there trip on the sidewalk a few days ago. If you walk over here, you'll definitely be safe.")

These action words when played in delivery are filled with intention and can get to my objective consistently. I can't just hope they cross the street. I have to use a technique so that I can be certain they will.

Once you've written your script, you can insert objectives and actions throughout, so that you have intentional performance choices happening all through the script.

Objective: What you want from your audience
Action: The intention behind your delivery is how you are going to get it.

- Tristan Harris spoke at TED2017. His talk, "How a handful of tech companies control billions of minds every day," is not only one of the most interesting talks, but it's also the perfect example of a speaker identifying the objective and using action to get it. He does this brilliantly. In order to get the attention of the audience right away, he engenders our interest by telling us he was a design ethicist at Google.

Objective: Get our attention
Action: Engender

- He also illuminates what we already know by using new language. We already know we are paying too much attention to social media feeds. But he illuminates this idea by using the words "race" and "persuasion."

Objective: Get us to think differently
Action: Illuminate

- He encourages us to think differently by sharing that ethical persuasion is when the goals of the persuader are aligned with the goals of the persuasion.
- He asks us to imagine a renaissance, which gets the audience to become excited about what's possible.

Objectives: Connect deeply to this idea and get selective with our attention
Actions: Encourage, employ, identify, empower

- Because each moment in his talk had clear intention based on his objectives and the actions he played, we trust him, we hear him, and we want to make a change because of this excellent performance. If he had just gone out there and talked about this idea, it would not have had the kind of impact that it does. He evokes feelings in us throughout the talk because everything he's doing is specific. He has a clear objective and uses several actions throughout the talk, to get his objective.
- Try using a clear objective today when you are out and about. See if you can get the cashier to smile. You can do that by complimenting her on her shirt. Or offer to take over so he can take a break. Or perhaps you can thank him or her.

Objective: Get someone to smile

Action: Compliment, offer, thank

- If one of these actions doesn't accomplish your objective, then move on to the next. This is the technique I teach my actors and speakers, which creates consistent and stellar performance every time. Your objective will remain the same. You must relentlessly go after it and if you are not getting what you want, change your action.
- If you want your spouse to take out the trash, you can nag, beg, or even seduce.

Using the Power of Your Voice with Objectives Offstage

Speaking is something we do every day. It's not limited to a stage. And I want you to consider the difference between having a stage, where the collective understanding is that you don't interrupt the speaker unless it's stand-up comedy and you are heckling, and being in a boardroom or at a dinner party, where there is a collective understanding that speaking is fluid and that everyone gets a chance.

Consider this: I have heard countless stories from women I've worked with, some professional female speakers, about either getting interrupted or simply never getting a word in when they are at a table with men. I love hearing these examples and analyzing them with my clients. I ask them why they didn't speak up. Or if they did, were they constantly interrupted? I try to help them determine if it was them or the men. It's usually a combination. I have witnessed this exact phenomenon in real-time during the recording of *The Big Talk Over Dinner*, a series I produced and directed where I invite people to have dinner with me while we have mindful conversations about hard topics. In the "Politics" episode, I invited three men and three women. This was already a tense topic, but what I was not prepared for was for the men to take over the conversation.

As the host of the series and the dinner, I consciously and graciously observed these three men often dominate (unintentionally) the conversation. What this taught me is that I can help in the future, if in the future, I give everyone at my table some tools and direction in advance. If the objective is to get any guest at any table to listen, you need an action. The objective also requires action. The actions I would have given my guests to use are push, stop, and command.

I would direct the women to Push. Push harder in getting their voice heard. This does not mean yell, fight, or cajole; it means push. When you can't get a door open, you apply more pressure and push until it opens. Same thing in this case—push gently with mild pressure until they are all ears.

And then Stop. Stop being polite and fearful of offending the guests at the table. When you stop your own chatter about the need to be polite or how you are going to be perceived, you will become the voice that is heard and excited to be collaborating with.

Finally, Command. Speak with a command so that when anyone begins to talk over you, you don't stop, waiver, or trail off. Command your presence, your voice, and your worth, so that if and when someone begins to interrupt you, they will see clearly in that moment they need to wait because what you have to say has value and needs to be heard. Push, Stop, and Command is gender neutral.

On stage or off, your voice is important, worthy, and of value. Do not allow it to be silenced by being polite.

I would love to invite us all to pay attention a little more when we are at a table, board or dinner, because all of our voices matter. *The Big Talk Over Dinner* also included the following episodes: "Gender," in which a transgender man, transgender woman, queer cisgender man, and cisgender woman were represented. The episode "Race and Immigration" included guests who were African American, biracial, Indian, Haitian, and Filipino American. Being conscious of inclusion, which brings diversity, is an important and integral part of having an influential voice. By having conscious conversations with people who are different from you, your voice becomes more powerful as a collective. The more every voice gets amplified, the more possible it becomes for the world to become a better place.

HOW TO GIVE AND RECEIVE FEEDBACK

Some people instantly take feedback as an attack. They sense this "attack" coming on before a word is even uttered. It usually comes with the question, "Can I give you some feedback?" or "I want to talk to you about your performance." Prominent psychologists and neurobiologists have found that our brains are hardwired to react to negative stimuli faster than to positive stimuli, which was originally necessary for our survival. Sensing an attack—and in this case, the fear of feedback—can trigger our body's natural fight-or-flight mode, increasing the amount of adrenaline released to the bloodstream, elevating reaction time and heightening our emotions. The experiences that trigger these reactions become etched into our brains so we can react to dangerous situations faster, which is why we tend to remember negative experiences more than positive ones.

Stanford Professor Carol Dweck's studies of the fixed and growth mindsets also provide valuable insights. According to her research, people with fixed mindsets view their skills as personal traits, while people with growth mindsets view their skills as malleable abilities that can be improved. When we associate abilities with a part of our identity, receiving constructive criticism can feel more like a personal attack. People with growth mindsets, on the other hand, are more likely to take risks and overcome obstacles by seeing failure as a signal to try harder, rather than a signal to give up.

So often, my speakers will present for a group of people a week or two before they are meant to deliver their TEDx or keynote. They go in without asking for specific feedback. What happens next is these people start giving their thoughts. It can be on the script, on the idea on the performance, how it starts, how it ends, the use of slides, blocking, or even what you're wearing. It becomes an opinion session disguised as feedback, and this is dangerous. At that time, every single belief you have in yourself and your talk goes away. Doubt, uncertainty, and insecurity fill you entirely, and you become lost in a sea of feedback you didn't ask for. Most importantly, you begin to believe those pesky lies. I have seen it happen over and over again. This is why you absolutely must be specific when you are delivering your talk one to two weeks before you are taking the stage.

Feedback Timeline: The Technique

A *few weeks out*, here's what to ask for.

> "Thank you so much for allowing me to deliver my talk today. Here is exactly what I'm looking for feedback on and nothing more. Thank you."

- How does the talk make you feel?
- Did you like the tempo of how I delivered it?
- What did you learn?
- What do you want to do afterwards?

By asking specific questions you are getting feedback on what you can actually address in a short amount of time. The *day before*, here is how you ask for feedback.

> "Today, I'm going to ask that you are simply a warm body for me. This means there is no room for feedback. I just want to have a human being to talk to."

If you are taking the stage *three months from now*, the kind of feedback you're asking for is different.

- Is the opening strong enough?
- Which story is strongest?
- Do you feel like the arc is clear?
- What emotional journey do you go on?
- Could the talk be too much about me and not enough about the audience?

These are questions that can serve you in the writing process, and if you have three months out, you have time to implement the changes by learning from this feedback.

Finally, when you are giving feedback to a speaker or anyone for that matter, always start with the positive before moving into the feedback. And ask before you jump in.

> "Are you available for some feedback? Great, first, I loved how you moved around in the space. The times you were still were super powerful. I am wondering if you have considered adding one more story about yourself. You have an incredibly interesting life and I'd love to hear more."

Both of these notes are framed positively. This is how you can give and receive feedback on stage or off.

If your head is spinning from this total technique package and you're eager to test them out, congratulations, you're definitely developing more of the influential mindset! Up next, we have the raw truth about pitching because after all, there's a lot to learn about crafting your intro and cultivating relationships. In the influential voice world, anyone may give you an offer you simply can't refuse.

Influential Voice Imprints

Being an influential voice means you know what you
want and how to get it.

An influential voice understands how to give and
receive useful feedback.

Being an influential voice means respecting differing
opinions and using dignified speech during conflict.

An influential voice is willing to do the
work to be heard.

Chapter 6

The Art of the Pitch

> "Those that don't got it, can't show it. Those
> that got it, can't hide it."
> —*Zora Neale Hurston*

KEY LESSONS

- Connect, authentically, with event organizers and speaker bureaus online before you pitch them.
- Being creative in how you follow up is how you stand out.
- Building relationships leads to landing stages.
- Becoming the go-to speaker means you are always in service to the audience and your community.
- Ask an organizer questions for your preparation, protection, and reputation before stepping on their stage.

After I worked on John Turturro's film *Romance and Cigarettes* as the choreographer, where I was awarded a Golden Thumb from

Roger Ebert (it's literally his gold cast thumb and I cherish it!), I thought I would have no trouble obtaining an agent. After all, I had just worked with most of the Hollywood greats. To my surprise, only one agent called me back, and the one who did put his feet up on his desk while eating McDonald's during our meeting. *Big mistake. Huge. (Anyone? Julia Roberts in* Pretty Woman.*)*

Being a choreographer is different from being a dancer. There are auditions for dancers all the time, and you just show up. But nobody has auditions for choreographers, as they get meetings and these meetings are set up by agents. I had to get creative. I had to stand out and earn my right to be called back. Since I couldn't get through the front door, I decided to go through the back door. I asked John Turturro to call a company of the best agents in the business for choreographers and directors on my behalf. Within hours, my phone rang, and they asked me to come into the office. I scheduled the meeting for the following week and promptly booked my flight, car, and hotel in Los Angeles. You see, I lived in New York City and they were based in L.A., but they didn't know that, nor did they need to. I wanted the meeting, I got it, and I was going to make it happen.

Once I got to L.A., I rehearsed the drive so that on the day, I would know exactly where I was going and how long it would take me to get there. I set myself up for success. The worst thing that could happen would be me getting lost, becoming flustered because I was late, and blowing the entire meeting. This is the kind of high-performance stuff I'm going to talk more about in the final chapter, our manifesto for high performers.

I showed up at the meeting, clear on my objective (to be signed on the spot) and how I was going to do that. I was going to charm, impress, and wow them. The meeting was amazing. And they said they were opening up a sister agency in New York City in a few weeks. How sensational is that? I didn't have to move to L.A., and I could still have the best representation.

They wanted to think about it and get back to me. I did not desire that as my objective, so I had to get even more creative. You see, your objective usually does not change, but your action needs to if you are not getting what you want. In thinking about how I could stand out from all the other potential clients they were signing, I knew that clearly, my body of work stood out. I wanted to go the extra mile though to show them I was meant to be part of their agency.

Instead of waiting for the phone call, I decided to be proactive in showing them who I was as a person. They needed to see me as more than just a choreographer giving them 20 percent on each Gap commercial I choreographed. I could have sent them an email, which in my mind is totally boring and, frankly, lazy. I could have sent them flowers, and what would have happened is that the flowers would either end up on one person's desk or in the lobby and people would simply admire the flowers.

Instead of those gestures, I sent them a cake. Because when you receive a cake, you can't eat it alone. You have to share it with everyone in the office, and when people ask, "Who sent you the cake?" and you respond, "Tricia, the choreographer we're going to sign," everyone would already be talking about me. Then I rise to the top of the conversation, and it shows them who I am as a human being. This is the kind of person they will want to work with. They signed me with the New York Agency immediately. This is the art of the pitch, and you do not need John Turturro to make a call for you. But you do need a strategy.

ALWAYS PITCHING: IT'S PART OF YOUR JOB

Did you know that Toastmasters International, a nonprofit educational organization that teaches public speaking and leadership skills through a worldwide network of clubs, has 357,000 members in 16,600 chapters? Why? Many members are in the corporate world and need the support for effective communication in sales transactions, relationship building, negotiation, conflict resolution, and presence and branding. Inevitably, some have their eyes on the big stages. Speaker bureaus, event planners, and organizations know that their speaker calls will be flooded with applicants from every direction. Among this fierce competition, you need to be creative and stand out, and that starts with relationship building. Consequently, the very important stages you desire to speak on should also be vetted. Surprise! You get to audition your organizer.

When you step into the role of speaker, it becomes your responsibility as an influential voice to live into this role. And it also means you are always pitching yourself. (Luckily we are going to cover being a high performer in Chapter 7.) I remind you, by sharing your powerful message, you have the potential to not only change but save a life.

Lead with, "I'm a speaker." Not only does the Universe need to know this, but also when you lead with this, everyone else will know too. By leading with authority as a speaker, you'll start to become known as someone who speaks for a living, creating credibility and visibility in the space.

Contact coordinators using the appropriate avenues like LinkedIn, Instagram, and other social media and make it clear you are available to speak at their next event and why that will serve them and their audience. Be sure to be specific and personal. Do not cut and paste your outreach. We know when you are doing that.

Attend conferences (virtual and live) and follow up with the organizer. Share with them how you loved the event, and how you can contribute to the next by serving the audience with your area of expertise. This needs to be a personalized email. You could even bring attention to the food, décor, or music and how it enhanced your experience. We want to know you were there and that you took the time to notice the little things as a kind human being. Cake. Remember the cake.

Ask for referrals. If you speak at an event, ask the organizer to make a referral to another organizer. There is nothing like being the keynote speaker who nails a conference and is on fire and ready to go. You are an easy sell to a colleague in that moment. Keep the fire burning.

Contact warm leads. Ask for support. Community is part of my values. I always say in my community you may be on stage alone but you are never by yourself. We need to support and uplift one another. Ask your colleagues for a referral. And when your mind goes into, "Oh, I don't want to bother them." Or "I can't ask for help," remember those are lies. The truth is, you are not bothering anyone, you are taking the proactive step in becoming an influential voice. And the other truth is that you can do anything, when you make the decision you will.

Offer yourself as a substitute to speakers you respect. There are a lot of speaking opportunities out there. And many speakers are fully booked up or may not want to travel all year round. Contact a speaker you respect who speaks on a topic you share and offer to step in when they are unable. Being unavailable to an organizer while offering up an alternative speaker whom you personally refer helps everyone. And keep that in mind. If you turn down an event, offer someone who can fill your shoes. You'll be respected in the field for this kind of generosity.

Relationships are how you are going to get the opportunity to use the art of the pitch. Remember the speaker I mentioned in Chapter 4, who pitched me the talk about his wife? He courted me for an entire year. He shared my articles on LinkedIn, he offered up his thoughts on my social media posts, and he was very respectful and authentic in his communication with me. When it was time for him to apply to TEDxLincolnSquare, he had already earned my trust, so it was an easy yes.

I'm going to go ahead and bet a cake on the fact that no one actually likes to write pitches, query letters (for books), or cover letters. Any takers? After all, you've written a rather substantial piece, the basis for pitching in the first place, and now you're wondering how in the influential world you are going to condense, whet an appetite, and make a substantial first impression. As is the case in physical performance and every other activity worth doing in this life, it takes rehearsal. It takes practice. Biceps curls and pliés over and over again. Here, I'm going to offer real-life examples along with my notes. Notice that there are both subtle and major differences because, seriously, one phrase or word can make the difference between a perfect pitch and a big "not yet."

PITCH COPY BEFORE AND AFTER

Example #1: Before

This is a pitch letter that I helped a client with. He has given me permission to share this with you, along with my explicit notes.

Dear Ms. Hamilton,

My name is James Lucas and I am the owner of Grape-cats. We sell high-quality vegan and eco-friendly clothing and accessories made without cruelty. I would love to speak at the VegFest. In my talk I describe my journey from a carnivore to a vegan through food and business. This journey includes my transition from eating meat to becoming vegan. Creating a vegan community and vegan blog. Working as a graphic designer to transitioning to owning a vegan clothing and accessories business.

Thank you,

James

_____

> *High-quality vegan and eco-friendly clothing and accessories made without cruelty.*

His tagline is great; it piques interest right away.

> *I would love to speak at the VegFest.*

He doesn't make it personal with why he wants to speak at VegFest.

> *In my talk I describe my journey from a carnivore to a vegan through food and business.*

This is all accurate information, but there is nothing passionate about it. We don't know why he would be the best person to speak at VegFest.

There is no bio or contact info. It's important to make sure there are links in the document, so that they don't have to take an extra step to try and find you.

Example #1: After

Dear Ms. Hamilton,

I'm a passionate and conscious vegan. I also own Grape-cats, where I sell high-quality vegan and eco-friendly clothing and accessories made without cruelty.

I'd be an excellent addition to your lineup of speakers. Not only can I share the journey I've gone on from carnivore to vegan, and the freedom, health and happiness it's created for me and my family, but I will also share my entrepreneurial journey of working in corporate, in offices and never being fully aligned with my beliefs. Being vegan and owning a cruelty-free company has given my life a deep purpose, and I want to share it with VegFest and the world.

I'm including my bio, contact information and links so that we can connect further. I look forward to hearing from you.

James Lucas

I'm a passionate and conscious vegan.

This introduction connects James to the VegFest community immediately. The event organizer doesn't have to wonder if he's a good fit.

I'd be an excellent addition to your lineup of speakers.

Be confident; sell yourself.

I share the journey I've gone on from carnivore to vegan, and the freedom, health and happiness it's created for me and my family, but I will also share my entrepreneurial journey of working in corporate, in offices and never being fully aligned with my beliefs.

Offer up your expertise while also being vulnerable and personal. It's not about your experience giving talks. It's about your passion on the topic and your ability to offer something of value to the audience.

Being vegan and owning a cruelty-free company has given my life a deep purpose, and I want to share it with Veg-Fest and the world.

End with why you are the person to take their stage.

Here is another example of a pitch from a client I worked with. She has also given me permission to share.

Example #2: Before

> "Be Whole—filling the emotional holes with love so you feel WHOLE again."

> Have you ever felt like you just weren't yourself? Or you felt incomplete and unfulfilled? You yearn for your life to be different, but you have no idea where it went astray let alone how to make it feel more complete. You want to reconnect to you and what you need...and want in life.

> Join Joanna as she discusses her journey from competitive athlete, to adrenal fatigue, starting over, and reconnecting to who she is and how her life's purpose became apparent.

> You will learn how holistic nutrition, Path To Heal energy work and essential oils help you to remember who you are at your core...You will find when you nourish the body, mind and soul, you can fill the emotional hurts from childhood and fall in love with your whole life.

She will also have her book, *Messages of Love & Inspiration for Every Moment* available.

Be Whole—filling the emotional holes with love so you feel WHOLE again.

"Be Whole—filling the emotional holes with love so you feel WHOLE again."

Be direct. This goes in circles and she uses Whole and hole too many times.

Being Whole Starts with Love

This is direct and something we want right now.

Have you ever felt like you just weren't yourself? Or you felt incomplete and unfulfilled? You yearn for your life to be different, but you have no idea where it went astray let alone how to make it feel more complete. You want to reconnect to you and what you need...and want in life.

Less is more. Get to the point.

Join Joanna as she discusses her journey from competitive athlete, to adrenal fatigue, starting over, and reconnecting to who she is and how her life's purpose became apparent.

"Apparent" is vague. Be specific.

You will learn how holistic nutrition, Path To Heal energy work and essential oils help you to remember who you are at your core...You will find when you nourish the body, mind and soul, you can fill the emotional hurts from childhood and fall in love with your whole life. She will also have her book, Messages of Love & Inspiration for Every Moment available.

Choose strong words when writing your pitch copy. It's got to make us want to sign up and get on board. See how "you will learn how" is passive? And it does not set Joanna up as the expert. Anyone could teach it. Also, "help you remember" is about a memory, not about an active state. She's not being direct enough about selling the book, and why not offer a special price? That always makes people feel special.

Example #2: After

Being Whole Starts with Love.

Have you ever felt like you just weren't yourself, incomplete and unfulfilled? You yearn for a different fulfilling life but have no idea how to make it feel more complete.

Join Joanna as she discusses her journey from competitive athlete, to adrenal fatigue, starting over, and reconnecting to who she is and how her life's purpose became crystal clear.

Joanna will introduce you to holistic nutrition, Path To Heal energy work and essential oils so you can be re-introduced to who you are at your core. When you nourish the body, mind and soul, you can fill the emotional hurts from childhood and fall in love with your whole life. Her book, Messages of Love & Inspiration for Every Moment will be available for a special price.

AMBITIOUS APPLICATIONS TO AN EVENT: MINI-GUIDE

So, you have a magnificent pitch that introduces you as an influential voice and your big idea that is personal and global? Great! Now, much more is needed to get noticed. At this point, you don't have to send a cake yet; however, once you've given the following due diligence, check back with me and I'll give you a few baker recommendations!

- Provide the event planner or organizer what you are giving the audience.
- List your idea, your value, your takeaways, and your learning objectives.
- Answer the questions being asked on applications, not what you want to answer.

Learning Objectives

Learning objectives, or learning outcomes, are statements that clearly describe what the audience will know and be able to do as a result of having attended the event or conference. Learning objectives must be observable and measurable.

Learning objectives should: focus on the audience, contain action verbs that describe measurable behaviors, and share an idea in a way that causes the audience to want to take immediate action in their life.

Verbs to consider when writing learning objectives

- *describe, write, discuss, explain, predict, apply, demonstrate, prepare, use, analyze, design, utilize, compile, create, compare*

These are active and tangible.

Verbs to avoid when writing learning objectives

- *know, understand, learn, appreciate, become aware of, become familiar with*

These are passive and do not get me excited about what I'm walking away with.

Example of well-written learning objectives

By the end of my time with you today, you'll be able to:

- Summarize basic hypnosis theory and technique in relationship to acute pain
- Recognize differences between spirituality and religion
- Apply a new way of thinking about simple handwashing with soap

How to Apply – It's an Art Form

I received hundreds of applications when I was the executive producer of TEDxLincolnSquare, Speakers Who Dare, and The Big Talk Academy Virtual Showcase. There is an art to applying. Here is what organizers and producers are looking for:

We want you to pitch an idea, not your business.

- Many people make this mistake. An idea is something the audience can potentially imagine for their own lives, thinking differently on the spot. Pitching me your business is selling me something.

The second thing to keep in mind is being clear on how your idea is related to the theme of the event. Themes I've seen are truth, making waves, and risk takers and change makers. When applying, be clear that your idea is somehow related to the theme of the event you are applying to. It also shows us that you did some research and have noticed this detail.

- One of my first speakers, discussed in Chapter 2, spoke about seeing the world through the eyes of her blind kids and raising awareness for this rare eye disease. She was clearly a risk taker and a change maker.

Organizers want you to make it clear that your idea is going to serve the community. The community in the room and the community as a population. How you tie that in is by saying it point-blank in the application.

- My idea of how I learned to see the world through the eyes of my kids will inspire your community to see things through the eyes of one another.

Four things will help get you chosen.
1. Give yourself the gift of time.
2. Choose an idea you are an expert on.
3. Remember, it's not about you.
4. Less is more.

1. Give yourself the gift of time.

Once you know the deadline, schedule time to write the first draft of the application. Reread the question more than once. Sometimes the questions are meant to send you in one direction, but it's your job to get to the source of what the organizer is asking. Be sure to answer the question they are asking, not what you want to answer.

Example:

> **What is the idea you will be sharing with our audience?**

> I'm going to share my ideas about global warming and ask the audience to make changes in their daily lives to hopefully reduce their carbon footprint, in turn making the world a better place.

Time could have helped this answer. This could be an example of an idea but the applicant didn't really understand the question, so they answered the question telling us they are going to ask us to do something. This answer is actually a call to action, not an idea.

A proper answer could be:

> I'm going to share specific ideas on exactly what changes we can make in our everyday lives in order to have the greatest impact on lessening or even eliminating our carbon footprint.

This answer is well thought and given the time it needed. And it's clearly an idea, which is what the organizers are looking for because the answer tells us we are going to walk away *with* something.

Now that you've filled out your application and reread the questions and thoughtfully written your answers, give yourself more time to revisit it one week before you submit. You will want to correct the typos you missed on the first pass and to make changes to sentence structure.

You may even change your mind about your big idea and want to write about something else. And if you do, good for you. You've just given yourself enough time to do that. When we step away from something we've written and come back to it, we see it with different eyes.

2. Always choose an idea you are an expert on.

Being a credible expert means you have lived this area of expertise. It does not require you to have a PhD at the end of your name, but you must know your stuff.

Be sure to apply with an idea that you are passionate about, but also an expert on. You must have credibility to talk about this idea. If you have a big complicated idea, back it up with science or statistics.

Let's say the application asks, **"What makes you the person to share this idea?"**

Here's one answer:

> Although I've never formally studied the art of
> seeing into the future, I was born into a family of

clairvoyants and therefore consider myself an expert on the subject.

This is an example of a noncredible applicant. There is not enough foundation to even consider this applicant. (And to be clear, I'm open to a lot of things. I have speakers in my community who channel. But this is a poor application.)

Here is a credible answer:

Not only have I been in the health and wellness industry for over twenty-five years, I've also worked directly with several doctors who specialize in Parkinson's disease that can show studies to prove that boxing does improve the motor function of early-onset Parkinson's patients.

This is clearly a credible expert.

Here is another tip on how to fill out a winning application.

3. Remember, it's not about you.

There are many wonderful inspirational keynotes and talks out there. Your talk should come from you and have your point of view. It should be made clear in the answer that you are passionate about the idea, and you are not making it about you and your needs.

Example:

Why are you passionate about this subject?

I have spent the last ten years working with in-mates on yoga and meditation while simultaneously working alongside psychologists on the effects these practices have had on the success rate of re-entry.

This is an excellent example of someone who is sharing why they are passionate about their idea without making it about them. *Here's another example:*

> Not only has my company been able to find jobs for people who have tried everything else, I've also been able to continue to grow my business into a seven-figure company, and I'm going to give a copy of my book to everyone at the end.

Never pitch your company or promote your book directly in an application.

4. Less is more.

Be clear, succinct, and specific. The ideas need to be expressed in a few words.

Example:

> **What idea are you communicating?**
>
> I'm going to talk about how when dogs live with us, they are so loving and sweet that they reduce stress and because we walk them, we get our workout. That is so healthy and ultimately leads to a longer life and can reduce blood pressure, just like going to the gym.

Phew, so long-winded! This is an example of how more doesn't work.

Here is an example of less.

> Having a dog can elongate a person's life and can potentially eliminate the need for blood pressure meds.

Less—this is how you can be effective in sharing your idea.

SPEAKER DOS AND DON'TS

Before you apply
- Get all your social media links ready and put them in one place.
- Write a one-hundred-word bio and make sure you update often.
- Make certain your website is up to date.
- Create a speaker reel, not an interview. If you don't have a reel, film yourself giving part of a talk, in more than one outfit and cut it together.
- Identify your organizational affiliations and keep them in one place.

Do – during the application process
- Follow and connect with the event organizers on social media.
- Post on social media about how excited you are about the opportunity to apply.
- Email a personal note thanking organizers for the opportunity.

Don't – during the application process

- Add event organizers on your email list. That's a sure way to not get chosen.
- Follow up too often. Once, to thank them, is enough.
- Ask them when they are going to be making a decision.

After – you land the gig

- Thank the organizers in an email.
- Post on social media how excited you are.
- Meet all the deadlines the organizers put into place. This is a sure way to be asked back.
- Overdeliver on all your promises.
- Ask the organizer for specs of the stage (dimensions).
- Ask the organizer if you'll be using handheld or lavalier microphones.
- Ask the organizer if you'll be being filmed and, if so, whether you can get a copy.
- Ask the organizer what the background of the stage looks like, so you can coordinate your wardrobe. If it's black, don't wear black.
- Ask the organizer how much time you get on the stage to rehearse ahead of time.
- Ask the organizer what kind of tech they provide, so you can either bring a thumb drive or send PowerPoint ahead of time.

BE THE SPEAKER WHO GETS ASKED BACK OVER AND OVER

You've booked your paid speaking gig, and you are super excited. Now, you are in the preproduction of the business of your speaking platform. Here are several things you can do to ensure you're going to make an impression before you even take the stage. And they will guarantee you're asked back the next year.

- Immediately follow up with a thank-you along with your book or some other tangible gift. This makes you stand out from the rest, as you learned at the top of this chapter.
- Connect with all the other speakers on LinkedIn and social media. (Remember community is part of my values and hopefully now part of yours.)
- Put your assistant in contact with the event organizer so they have a point of contact going forward. If you do not have an assistant, create an Assistant@yourname.com email address so people will think you do.
- Begin posting on social media and tagging the event.
- Schedule alerts in your calendar to remind you to connect or collect details.
- Plan out the day for yourself, leaving time to be social with the organizer. Don't leave right after you speak. Stick around long enough to take photos and connect.

- And a few days later, send a gift. Yes, another gift. Being generous is not hard and so important. Follow up asking for feedback on how you could have improved and communicating that you are available anytime they ask.

VETTING: IT'S CRITICAL!

At the local level, leaders, authors, and influencers are applying to countless events in the hopes of not only being paid, but also capturing excellent video to submit to future conferences. Good reels and respected stages give speakers instant credibility, along with the potential for massive visibility.

When vetting organizers, ask these five questions:

How long have you been producing this event?

If the organizer is a first timer, you have nothing to go on in terms of their ability to pull off a great event. If the organizer has not produced an event before and you are willing to take a risk on them, be sure to ask how many months they will spend planning the event. Be sure to obtain photos of the venue ahead of time. If the organizer has produced the event before, ask for the list of speakers from the past event and reach out to them to ask about their experience. For example, did they feel supported or were they micromanaged?

Do you have a team in place?

This is important because if they think they can do this alone, they are mistaken. Any organizer who has no team will be unable to do anything well and might ask you to put the stage together with them the day of the event. If they do have a team in place, be sure to ask who they are and what their roles are. When you know that you have a stage manager, lighting designer, tech director, videographer, editor, house manager, and volunteers, you are going to be taken care of.

How many speakers are you curating?
Asking this question can give you a sense of what the audience will be expecting. For example, you likely do not want to be in a line-up of thirty speakers because if you're last, the audience will have speaker fatigue, and you'll be talking to a bunch of zombies. If you choose to say yes to an event with a lot of speakers, ask to go first in the lineup. Conversely, if there are only a few speakers, this can be a red flag, too. Only a few speakers could mean other speakers turned the organizer down. Look for a good middle ground.

Do you use a professional videographer and sound engineer?
As a producer, I know that the videos are paramount for a speaker's ongoing success. You have to be able to show what you are capable of. This is why I've found it's essential to always ask about the quality of video you should be expecting. If you want to be represented well, make sure the video quality is excellent. You can also watch videos from past events. If the videos look good, it's likely the event will have quality videos in the future.

Why are you producing this event?
This question is critical because I've observed that many event organizers make the event about them, not the speakers. What you should look for is an organizer who says, "It is my passion to

support incredible speakers and their ideas, so that their messages can be heard all over the world." You want to avoid organizers who call the event "theirs" and who want to remove your point of view from your talk. If they try to rewrite your talk to sound like their voice, you are doing a disservice to yourself and your audience.

Work with an organizer who is going to elevate you and the other speakers along the way. Identifying a big idea, crafting a speech, and getting it performance-ready by being totally off book (memorized) is not easy and is very time-consuming. I want your experience to be transformational and inspired. There are plenty of amazing events out there run by outstanding producers. And by doing this kind of due diligence and requiring an organizer to apply to you first, you will save time, money, and potential heartache.

CLUES WE LOOK FOR

When I'm accepting applications for my events, I'm looking for many things. It always starts with the big idea, but then I want to get to know the person a little more. When I'm casting a show, it's the same thing. If I'm going to be spending months with this person, I want to like them. I also desire to work with people who are kind and care about the community; not all organizers have these values, or need to, but they just happen to be mine. I will ask very specific questions to weed out anyone who might be difficult to work with, ego driven, lazy, or unable to follow directions. And here is how I do that.

When I ask you to share why this is the talk of your life, and you answer with a few words like, "It's important to share it," this tells me two things: You have not really thought about it on such a deep level. Second, as a result I have no choice but to conclude that you don't care about this event, since you may use canned answers in all your applications.

When I ask you to tell me a little more about yourself and you cut and paste your bio into the answer form, it tells me one of two things: either your assistant filled it out for you, or you are lazy.

This question is meant to connect me to you. At auditions, I always look at the special skills at the bottom of a résumé before how many Broadway shows you've done. I almost cut a dancer who ended up being in *Broadway Varietease,* a burlesque show I directed and choreographed in New York City, because I didn't look at her special skills right away. She twirled batons, and that is how the casting of her baton twirling act in my show happened. It took down the house every show. And we have gone on to become dear friends. All because of her special skills.

If you just cut and paste your bio, you do not give us as organizers an opportunity to be inspired, intrigued, or excited to choose you.

When I ask you to submit by the deadline and you email me directly with an excuse as to why you didn't make the deadline, it tells me two things: it's about you and will stay about you during the process, and you do not prioritize things that you care about.

And finally, when you submit a video that is longer than what I've asked for, it tells me two things: you don't follow directions, and I can't trust you to perform in my show at the length of time given because you think you can do whatever you want.

When you are in full integrity in your pitches and you are really giving the organizers what they are actually asking for, not what you want to answer, then you will stand out and your powerful voice will have a platform for giving to the world.

Time to take a pulse check on your influential voice evolution! How are you feeling? If you are feeling the rise of heat from nervousness and anticipation, the steady hand of knowledge and expertise guiding you to your own wisdom, and unbridled curiosity as to where your new consciousness will take you, you're ready for the manifesto. Trust me—it will be hard to turn back to old ways at this point; you're in control of how big and bold you want to be. And you won't be the same.

Influential Voice Imprints

An influential voice never makes it about them.

Being an influential voice means you are
a credible expert.

An influential voice respects the art and asks for
what they want.

An influential voice is always in action of service, for
the good of humanity.

Chapter 7

Manifesto of a High Performer

⣿⣿⣿⣿⣿⣿

"If we practice being spectacular long enough,
spectacular will become our way of being."
—*Robin Sharma*

KEY LESSONS

- Be accountable for your daily behavior toward being an influential voice.
- Speaking requires the same level of training as being an elite athlete.
- Gratitude and life design elevate your vibration, pandemic or not.
- High performance requires boundaries around the people in your life.
- A daily practice of self-care is not optional; it's mandatory.

You have to earn the right to be the voice. You have to keep showing up and moving the story forward. Overnight success takes decades. You have to want it bad enough. You have to have a white-hot desire and burn the image in your mind.

We are not entitled as speakers. We are not entitled as human beings. We must earn the right to be the voice. We must earn the right to be the ally. We must earn the right to ask you to buy our services and goods. We must not have expectations, and we must be detached from any and all outcomes related to speaking and using the voice. When you speak your truth and share your important message, it's very important that you let go of and detach from what is going to happen. Will they like me? Will I stutter? Will they yawn? Will I have impact? That makes it about you.

It is our job to make it about the world and the people we are serving. By showing up consistently and by having the courage to be visible and to be willing to be criticized, to be willing to have haters and receive bad comments, that is when you earn the right to be the voice. Showing up consistently on social media, showing up consistently at networking events. Showing up consistently for yourself and for your family and your community. And this goes back to Chapter 1. When you're clear on your purpose, mission, and values, then you understand who you are and how you can show up consistently.

You must be the same person every time. Again, you have to earn the right to be the voice. You have to be willing to roll up your sleeves and do the work, so that people begin to hear you, so that people begin to pay attention. And you have to keep the story moving.

KEEP YOUR STORY MOVING

I've talked about hearing no all the time in my career. I've heard the word no a million times. If I had let this little word, made up of two letters, worth only two points in Scrabble, stop me, I wouldn't be right here showing up for you, writing this book for you. I wouldn't have the wisdom to share so you can be the influential voice.

But here is the link to visibility and consistency. Keeping the story moving means acknowledging the no as a not yet and moving on. It means acknowledging the challenge as an opportunity and continuing to move forward. The forward momentum is how you are going to have the ripple effect that you need. Everyone knows slow and steady wins the race; there are no overnight successes. It takes decades to have the foundational success that will hold you and all of your followers and all the people you are mentoring up.

If you rapidly spread out a foundation built on surface-level thoughts and ideas, what is going to happen when all of a sudden, a million people want to hear your important message? You're all going to just fall to the bottom. It's really important that you create that solid foundation of integrity with purpose, mission, and your values so that when that success hits, your structure is solid and in place.

Also, we have to want this bad enough. If you go back to the vision, what is your vision? What's the white-hot desire that is burned in your mind?

Mine: *Making the world a better place by elevating speakers like you.*

Have the courage to be visible. Be visible in integrity. Continue to show up every day. And let's talk about how!

I have been an artist for three decades, and I have also been an entrepreneur that entire time. And that has required grit and massive trust. Being an artist and an entrepreneur are pretty much both a roll of the dice, according to most paradigms. "Maybe you'll be one of the lucky ones who are successful." Being lucky is the lie. Being smart is the truth. Let's think about the significance of this combo when it comes to responsibility, commitment, and accountability: I'm my own boss every hour of the day. I create and coach others whether or not I'm fueled with motivation and inspiration. I need a schedule and I need to maintain it as if it were life or death. No matter what your livelihood or schedule is, there is a component here that you can relate to. We are typically accountable for results somewhere in a performance chain. In my case, I understand that my clients and creative partners rely on me to show up fully on every occasion for moving our story along. Results are a direct reflection of who I am and how I show up, walk, dance, or jump around in this world.

Does all this signify mile-high pressure sometimes? Or all of the time, you mean? Yep. But here's the satisfying sweet spot: success. And I don't mean traditional symbols of success in the form of titles, accolades, and awards, though these things are important and I'm not understating any component of achievement. As an influential voice, I'm referring to the deeper, delicious success of doing everything I could to create change and have impact. Impact is paramount to me—and all influential voices I help to cultivate.

Here, I want to talk to you about high performance, not just one activity or one project. Specifically, my high performance, and I give deep respect to the "world's leading high-performance coach," Brendon Burchard, but that's not what I'm going to be touching on. I want to talk to you about my high performance that is consistently practiced as a lifestyle. Don't be scared! Your high performance won't have the same face as mine or your favorite Olympian.

THE HABIT LOOP OF SUCCESS *HAS* TO BE DAILY

Joe and I have two cats, Lola and Bella: one that is quite the agile performer for everyone or no one to see, sprinting and hopping around, asking to be picked up with bellowing meows, and the other, more of a performer in her charm, luxuriating and lounging, making constant and deep eye contact, communicating to me that it's time for her to be on my lap. They're both so darned consistent. Every single day.

I am a highly productive person and because I've been asked about how I accomplish so many things and so many different things, I am going to share my tips to help you achieve massive amounts of success by improving your level of performance. Being a beacon of light in the world using your voice for good takes the same kind of training as an elite athlete.

I have a lot to accomplish in this world and we never know when it's the final curtain, so I'm going to use *every day* to reach my highest potential.

Anyone who knows me knows it's my policy to not go out during the week. I go to bed between 7:00 and 7:30 p.m. every day, even on the weekends. If I do go out on a weekend night, I still get up at the same time. In the city that never sleeps, no one said this would be easy. But it's the city that always dreams too, and my ultimate dream was, and is, world impact, so New York gets me! This consistency in my sleep pattern gives me the energy and focus to develop shows, make documentaries, produce events, and work with some of the most elite clients.

You must get enough sleep. This sleep becomes twice as meaningful when you have a daily practice. It's important to identify your daily practice. What you're doing with the first several hours of your morning when you get up. Going right to your phone, computer, or your email is not high performance. It is going to agitate you, prevent you from being creative, and even make you nauseous. It does. You may have ignored that feeling in your gut before, hellbent to look and read anyway, but it's there, inside your body.

Dr. Victoria L. Dunckley, a frequent contributor to *Psychology Today,* writes extensively on screen time stressing and detuning the body clock, brain chemistry, and reward pathways, as well as how tech addiction can actually damage the brain's frontal lobe. She has also shared how an electronic fast can reset and resynchronize the nervous system, which I can definitely raise my hand from experience and tell you that it does. We live and work by it, but given the science, is this *really* what you want to put your body through first thing in the morning? Not if you are a high performer.

Understand what you need in a daily practice.

For example, because of COVID-19, as of this writing, and because I live in New York City, and it's extremely tense here, I have come to realize that in order to be my best for clients and for myself, I literally need six hours of self-care. This need was borne out of the pandemic; however, I'm planning to maintain this kind of self-care going forward. From 4:00 a.m. to 10:00 a.m., it's all about me. This may seem unreasonable, and I am very clear that not everyone has six hours to spend on themselves. I in no way belittle the many parents out there who have a lot of responsibilities and are unable to take six hours to do what you need and wish to do for yourselves. I do not have children and I work for myself, so the privilege I have is not lost; however, you have to make time for yourself. You have to choose *you* some of the time. Even if it's five minutes. I know you can find five minutes to do you. In fact, if you are reading this now, you are taking at least five minutes for yourself and with this book, and for that, I am in gratitude.

Doing me means hydration, working out, meditation, self-study, and organizing my office so that everything is in its place. If things are out of place in your home, on your desk, in your workspace, things will be out of place in your mind. Organizing yourself, understanding how much self-care you need, is a nonnegotiable. I write in a journal every single morning. I write what I'm thankful for and then I design my day. Thankful can be for things that have not happened yet. Thankful for the new speakers I have the privilege of directing. Thankful can be for the coffee my husband, Joe, made me. Thankful for the sweet meows of Lola and the gremlin purrs of Bella. It is what I'm thankful for today and what I will be thankful for tomorrow. I want you to get serious about what I'm proposing. Dr. Joe Dispenza's teachings in the book *Breaking the Habit of Being Yourself* are all about being in gratitude and receivership for what has already happened. That is the kind of grateful I'm talking about. I'm thankful for what I see in the future, as if it's already happened. Like you reading this book; it happened while I was writing it, and I'm thankful for you and have yet to meet you. That's powerful and all part of being a high performer.

After I'm in gratitude, I design my day. What do I want my day to look like?

- I will be highly productive.
- I will serve my clients at the highest level.
- I will have a positive impact and make a difference energetically in the world every single day.

Even if I am sheltered in place during COVID-19 in New York City, how I show up will energetically create a ripple effect in the world. What I do every single day to show up at the highest possible version of myself to have an impact is no joke.

If we talk about daily practice, that is what you need to do every morning to be your best self.

If monthly practice, that means breaking down what you will accomplish in a month to set yourself up for success. Achieving these tasks will create your habit of meeting your goals. I don't mean that your practice can be setting a low bar or choosing goals you know you will achieve. Always choose goals that are bigger than you can imagine. In the daily picture meet your goals and create those successful habit loops. And in the big picture do not create goals that you know you will accomplish. I want you to reach beyond, because I know these bigger goals are waiting for you to create them.

Regarding a yearly practice: how do you want to show up for the next year of your life? By committing in that way, that increases the stakes that you will show up every day. If I have a vision of what my year looks like, which is training thousands of speakers from all over the world in the Big Talk Academy (www.thebigtalkacademy.com), that means I am always going to get up at 4:00 a.m., so I have the brain space to create new content, and always show up every single day at my highest level, because my yearly practice requires me to do that.

What do you need to do every single day to show up fully? To serve your community, your family, your clients at the highest level? Ask yourself: What is my yearly practice? Paint this picture. See what it looks like and feels like and be this person *every single day*.

If you make a commitment to a client and you keep that date, that session, and you show up on time and 1,000 percent and completely focused and dialed in, you need to have that same commitment for yourself. If you are scheduling work time for yourself and you let social media slide into the place of it, you have broken a commitment to yourself and you're one step farther away from being that influential voice. When you make a commitment to your family, your team, yourself, be in full integrity at all times. Back to values. When you are consistent and this behavior becomes second nature, you increase your productivity. You increase your ability to set yourself up for success.

Starting my day with the same routine keeps a habit loop of success in place for me. And trust me, lists galore are involved. The reason lists are important to me is that I need space in my brain to be creative. Whether it's writing a show or a talk or strategizing with a speaker or directing an actor, I need my brain to have space to think. I do not allow my brain to be filled up with tasks for the day or the to-do list of the week. I have a daily, a weekly, and an ongoing to-do list.

The act of remembering takes away from the act of being creative.

My daily list of goals is on a three-by-five note card. Sometimes I need two. Mostly, I keep it limited to one side of the three-by-five card. When I accomplish the goal, I cross it off. This is the most satisfying experience, as I win each time that I cross off meeting a goal for the day; this reinforces my own success.

The weekly list is what I want to accomplish by the end of the week. I allow those tasks or goals to be fluid throughout the week, whether it's writing an article, planning an event, or developing a new podcast concept. This fluidity takes any pressure off and allows me to move from the daily list of goals to the weekly as time frees up.

There are 224 things on my ongoing list. These are things like ideas for a new show, new camera equipment that I may want to invest in, a trip to Greece—these are the things I don't have to get to right now. But I don't want to forget about them or leave them untapped, so I write them all down.

Because I write everything down, I am free to be my highest level of creative self. Of course, the daily routine is governed by behaviors beyond lists and keeping my gallon container full of H_2O, and perhaps the most complicated for a lot of people—boundaries, as high performers may also be unapologetically social, loving creatures and people pleasers.

BEHAVIOR DICTATES PERFORMANCE

I'm just going to say it because we're all human and I've seen and experienced a lot: if you've had bad behaviors for the last ten years, you absolutely must put on the brakes, revisit how to get out of those behaviors, and create new ones. Do it now. It can't wait. This is about rewiring our brains, learning to think differently, and having a vision that it is more important than any behaviors or any other ways of showing up in the world. There is only one way: as a high performer.

Questionable behavior that counters your highest performance is not just avidly partying on Friday and Saturday nights. It can be the undercover things you do: how much water you drink, what kind of food you eat, if you're conscientious about supplements, washing your hands, exercise, and meditation. When you bring behaviors into your life and you set yourself up for success as a high performer, your voice is going to have more reach. You are going to be consistently showing up at the highest possible level. Only when you do that does the power of your voice come through in a way that will impact. Because you are living your life at the highest possible level. Because you are highly productive.

Writing a talk takes a really long time. It is not easy. If you don't have your mindset clear, if you don't understand how important consistency is with getting up every morning at the same time, going to bed to sleep at the same time, making sure you are hydrated by drinking a gallon of water (I mean a gallon, yes, *a gallon*) every day, making sure you understand how you perform with certain kinds of foods you eat, you won't experience your influential voice and neither will others.

- What are you going to do today to identify a questionable habit?
- Who are you going to ask to be accountable for this new habit implementation?
- How are you going to stay consistent with your new and high-performance habits?

A TALE IN HIGH PERFORMANCE

I had the privilege of a unique and remarkable dance career, having toured all over the world as I mentioned earlier, dancing at the Paris Opera House, the Vienna Opera House, Portugal, all over Europe, and at Lincoln Center. I realized that I was limited in my impact by the number of people in the theater and the length of my dance. I realized that I wanted to do more. I wanted a lasting legacy that was outside of being a performing artist. In order to move on and start having that kind of impact and working with people that would have more of a ripple effect, that meant working with people in theater, film, and television so I could work with more people, and all those people would have a ripple effect.

I needed closure before getting to the next level. I aimed to create a concert where I would showcase all of the solos and choreographers that I had worked with over the twenty-plus years of my career as a dancer. And I had just become a choreographer, so I wanted to create a solo show where I was showcasing all the works I had ever done. I spent nine months preparing. Just like having a baby, giving birth, so I wanted to take the time to do it right and have that incubation period be right.

High performance?

I did everything I possibly could to set myself up for success on that stage. I scheduled all the rehearsals in advance, so I knew exactly when I would be going to the theater for nine months—not just frequency but what time on those days. I booked the theater. I hired my team.

I started working with a director, who happens to be my husband now (never think you can direct yourself, ever!). I did everything I could in advance so that I didn't have to worry about anything. I could just be the dancer once the rehearsal period started. I also hired an assistant and taught her all the dances so I could watch her do these dances and get a sense of the arc of the through line of this show called *Dining Alone*. I also knew very much that it would be hard for me to warm myself up because I would be very nervous. I was carrying an hour and a half solo show by myself, so I hired a yoga teacher to come to the studio every evening to give me a private yoga class, so I did not have to think about warming myself up. She was doing it for me. I was able to be in my body and focus on what was happening with the show.

I also understood that I needed to have my costume designer who would be dressing me and undressing me in the dressing room with me because I would do a dance and then I would come off stage and sit down in order to give my quadriceps a rest and all the lactic acid that was building up a chance to flow out so that I would have enough strength and endurance to do the next dance.

I would sit there, let her undress me; I would stand up, she would redress me; and then I would sit back down, have water, and then I would go out and do my next number. I also understood exactly what I needed to eat because I started rehearsing what I needed to eat months in advance so I knew what my body would do with carbohydrates versus proteins. I repeated what worked every single day leading up to this one-woman show.

I also knew that I had to have the proper mindset: I'm meant to do this. I deserve to do this. I am absolutely the person to do this. This is a culmination of my career. And I spent nine months creating what I like to refer to as my "Zen sand sculpture" inspired by a group of Tibetan Buddhist monks from the Drepung Loseling Monastery in India. To promote healing and world peace, they travel the world creating incredible mandalas using millions of grains of sand. For days or even weeks, the monks spend up to eight hours a day working on one mandala sand painting, pouring multicolored grains of sand onto a shared platform until it becomes a spectacular piece of art. When they're finally finished, they step back...and they wipe it all away. That is exactly what happened with *Dining Alone*, my one-woman dance show. It was an incredible creation and one of my proudest moments. And when it was over, it was *over*. I wiped it all away. I needed to have more impact.

In terms of high performance, I did everything I could to set myself up for success. If I had not gone through this painstaking process and preparation, I would not have reached all those people in the theater. If I had not set myself up for success, I would have been worrying today about what I could have done better instead of concerning myself now with how to mentor as many influential voices, like you, as possible.

BOUNDARIES MATTER
(IT'S TIME TO BELIEVE THIS)

As influential voices, we must draw clear boundaries around everyone in our life. If there is anyone in your life preventing you from having your voice, you're going to have to cut them out. You're going to have to create boundaries that are going to make it clear to these people that they cannot get in the way of your white-hot vision. That they cannot reflect anything poorly onto you that will potentially dim your light, that they cannot take your time when your time is extremely valuable, when you are working on having an influential voice.

If you are having coffee dates with people who do not support or elevate or enlighten your potential as an influential voice, then it is time to stop having coffee with those people. This is serious business. Spending time with people who bring you down, suck your energy, and take advantage of your time has to end. Boundaries are paramount—for your family, friends, colleagues. Choose to spend time with people who are only going to support you and your desire to be an influential voice.

YOUR SCIENCE FOR SUCCESS IS IN THE SYSTEMS

If you'd rather talk about systems or technology because you're a softie who's not ready to draw clear boundaries around people, I get it. I will indulge you. I have systems for everything. (Note: The following software brands are not sponsors; I'm only referring to them for frame of reference. There are tons of other software out there that can support you fully as well. These just happen to be the ones that I use to support my high performance.)

Routine Email Content (Don't Skip This Section)
If you want to be an influential voice, you have to *talk* to people, and that includes a weekly newsletter. Sharing your valuable ideas and providing ongoing value *consistently* is the key to being a high performer. I batch my newsletters three months in advance. By doing this, it frees me up to work on other things, like editing a documentary or creating a new program for my speakers, like The Art of The Big Talk Masterclass. And when someone responds to an email you wrote three months ago, it's a welcome surprise!

Schedule a day out in advance where you block off four hours. Set a goal for yourself and then decide to finish. Make the decision that you *are* going to write three months of emails and do it. Allow me to remind you that when you find yourself scrolling through Facebook, you are wasting your precious time and allowing distractions to get in the way of your purpose, mission, and how to change and even save lives. Being an influential voice is something that you have to always embody, not just when you are on stage. Setting and achieving daily goals is part of the high performer equation.

Tame the Email Horde!

Did you know that about three hundred billion emails are exchanged on our collective information highway *every single day*? How many of those do you receive?

Organizing email can eat into your performance time. And opening your Gmail account can throw anyone into a state of panic or paralysis. I use SaneBox to filter all my emails into sorted folders. I have reduced online shopping by 100 percent, and I have eliminated distractions from colleague newsletters completely. If a colleague really wants me to attend their event or buy their product, they will email me personally and that will go to my personal email because I filter it in.

Simultaneously, with scheduling, to be highly productive, you have to stop going back and forth with people in emails around when you are going to meet up. Set up your calendar and share the link. This will save you an immense amount of time and energy. Use an intake form (in the software, I use Acuity) so that you know who the person is, full name, how they found you, and what they desire to talk about. Always do your homework before your call. You have an opportunity to be an influential voice with this person, so if you show up and have no idea who they are or why they wanted to meet, it's a waste of your time and theirs.

Manage Time Wisely

Determine how long you are going to work on something and stick to it. Your time is precious, and you deserve your own respect. If you don't finish it, stop and add time to the next day. You don't let your clients go over, so why would you let yourself break those boundaries? If you find that you are inspired, like I was when writing this book for you, extend the time for an additional hour and reevaluate your day.

No matter what you are doing that requires sitting, stand up every hour. Just. Do. It. I don't have to tell you this because that's what I rely on Mayo Clinic for: research has linked sitting for long periods of time with a number of health concerns. They include obesity and a cluster of conditions—increased blood pressure, high blood sugar, excess body fat around the waist, and abnormal cholesterol levels—that make up metabolic syndrome. Too much sitting overall and prolonged periods of sitting also seem to increase the risk of death from cardiovascular disease and cancer.

Do not schedule clients or calls back to back. This is going to burn you out and prevent you from being a full version of yourself for each call.

Schedule play time. It's important that just like recovery from working out, you schedule recovery time into your day, week, and year. Whether it's a walk, a date, or a weekend getaway. Recovery is needed so you can be a high performer and, ultimately, the influential voice.

Passwords and Peace of Mind, Not Memory

When I moved my entire life into the vault that is LastPass, my anxiety around passwords was eliminated. How much time do you spend looking for, worrying about, and trying to remember passwords? Do yourself a huge favor and create one master password that will give you access to a safe place that houses everything. You can also share the links with your team so they have access to places like your Facebook account without them seeing the passwords. It's a revelation!

No Texting

I'm not a fan of texting. I find it to be an extremely lazy way of communicating. It's also a dangerous way of communicating. How many times have you worried you've either offended someone or been offended because you can't distinguish tone? Not to mention, I don't want to have my phone congested with tons of texts from clients and speakers. This is why I use Voxer, a great way for me to leave a quick voice memo to my team about something I might need right away. It's also a great place for me to cheer on a speaker who's doing wonderful things.

Client Zone

I have a folder for each client. In the folder are notes from our last meeting and what our goals are together. In order to serve my clients at the highest level, I schedule time for myself in advance to review these notes and create an agenda for our meeting. In order to keep my brain space clear, so I can be super creative with the client, doing this preproduction guarantees that my full focus and attention are spent serving my client on the call.

Deadlines

I give deadlines because if I'm waiting on a speaker or an actor for a headshot, it slows down my delivery time to my graphic designer and then slows down my ability to send out the PDF the day I want. That kind of waiting is messy and annoying. Brain clutter can be eliminated by giving deadlines, allowing for the creative brain space. How you can do this is by simply making it very clear that you are "looking forward to thanking" the person for this deliverable "by the end of the day."

The Priceless Thank-You

Thank-yous are free. But nothing could be more valuable. I thank my team daily. Whether it's Voxing my appreciation or sending a quick note in the mail (yes, old school), I want my team to know without a doubt that their work is invaluable to me. I have spent many hours training my team and if they don't feel supported, valued, and cared for and motivated to juggle all the balls of my business with grace and consistency, it would take hours and hours of my time to manage all the moving parts and ultimately take me away from being the creative visionary. Give thanks, and give thanks often.

Nonnegotiables

Know yours. Working out, meditation, and integrity are mine. I live by integrity and alignment. Then consistent eating habits. I eat lots of cruciferous veggies and avocado. I drink tons of water. Consistency and boundaries are the big ones for me. Determine what your big ones are and decide to commit to them every day. And if a voice pops into your head and says, "You are being selfish. Who do you think you are for taking so much self-care time?" I want to remind you, we are not playing small here. Being an influential voice is serious and urgent, and you do not have time to second-guess yourself or what you need. Also, you do not need anyone in your life who second-guesses you either. I repeat. We are not playing small here.

Commit to Yourself

During the pandemic, I decided to create a YouTube Channel. I was advised that if you post new content for four solid months, Monday through Friday, the algorithm will push your channel to the top of your niche and your subscribers will organically start climbing to the thousands. I took on the challenge. No professional hair and makeup, no fancy studio—we were sheltering in place with no salons for root touch-ups, if you know what I mean. We could all see what states were opening up first based on who would come show up with a haircut. New York was closed for four months, but I still kept the commitment to myself that I was going to do this. I was going to shoot eighty episodes about the art of public speaking for *The Big Talk* on YouTube.

Was it hard? Yes! Was it stressful? Absolutely. (I quickly learned I may not have eighty outfits.) Did some days feel like a grind? It was work, and it was worth it. I created thirty unique videos in two days in April, we launched on May 4, 2020, and I had the rest of the videos shot by June 30. I kept my commitment to myself because I want to serve as many people as possible who desire to have an influential voice. As I'm writing this book, we are in month three of the experiment. I hope you'll be one of the thousands who are going to be subscribing!

Self-Study

I have always put myself in a room with people who know more than me. I want to be pushed beyond what I already know. I like the term *beyond*. Remember when I asked you in the beginning to envision goals beyond what you thought to be naturally achievable? I want to be questioned beyond what I believe to be true. And I want to keep learning. I also start every day by studying. Some of the books that have inspired me on my journey to be here with you today include:

- *Breaking the Habit of Being Yourself* by Dr. Joe Dispenza
- *Think and Grow Rich* by Napoleon Hill
- *Metahuman* by Deepak Chopra
- *White Fragility* by Robin DiAngelo
- *The Millions Within* by David Neagle
- *How to Be an Antiracist* by Ibram X. Kendi
- *The 10X Rule* by Grant Cardone
- *Sassafrass, Cypress & Indigo* by Ntozake Shange
- *Trust* by Iyanla Vanzant
- *The Science of Getting Rich* by Wallace D. Wattles
- *The Compound Effect* by Darren Hardy
- *I Heart My Life* by Emily Williams

- *The Perfection Detox* by Petra Kolber
- *The Art of Making Dances* by Doris Humphrey
- *An Actor's Companion* by Seth Barrish
- *Pitch Anything* by Oren Klaff
- *E-Squared* by Pam Grout
- *Profit First* by Mike Michalowicz
- *The Collaborative Habit* by Twyla Tharp
- *Identity Leadership* by Stedman Graham

Giving Back

Being an influential voice means speaking out, stepping into your power, and also being conscious about giving back. A high performer knows the power in spreading the wealth in terms of knowledge and financial means.

In relation to knowledge, I had the immense pleasure of mentoring a young woman named Emma Cullen. She came to me with the desire to be mentored in her senior year in high school, during the application process of getting into colleges for acting. We spent an entire school year working on the craft of acting, script analysis, and audition techniques. It was one of the most fulfilling experiences I've had in my career. The reason why is that I was able to witness this young girl step fully into her purpose as a young woman, who was no longer apologizing for desiring to become "an actor." It was absolutely possible for her and when she began to own that reality (truth), and own her influential voice, Emma developed into an exceptional actor and also recognized her own leadership role in the world, so much so that I put her on my stage, Speakers Who Dare, to talk about how summer camp taught her about leadership.

Giving back to someone has a ripple effect you cannot foresee. In Emma's own words, which I consider to be highly influential:

> The thing about a voice is that we all have one. Finding it implies that at one point I had lost it, when in fact it was always there—I had just spent so much of my life suppressing it. I've always had dreams, opinions and ideas, but I felt that what I had to offer was not worth sharing... I was dreaming too big, I was too young to make a difference, and the overwhelming fear that I could say something wrong. It wasn't until I was eighteen that I realized if I didn't take action, the life I want would pass me by. So, I announced that I wanted to be an actor, which came as a surprise to pretty much everyone... except me. I had been thinking it and feeling it for years, but I never said anything. Enter Tricia Brouk. Tricia was more than an acting coach and more than just a teacher. She was and is a mentor to me. She taught me dreams are supposed to be big, that young voices like mine are the voices of the future, and that I will, in fact, make many mistakes.
>
> During our time together, Tricia asked me to do many things for which I felt I was in no way

qualified. She asked me to be an understudy in her musical when I neither sing nor dance; she asked me to talk on politics before I really understood my own stance on issues; she encouraged me to give a speech on empowering young girls when I still felt like one myself. I spent many nights prior to these events worrying about what I would say, and many nights after these events thinking about what I wished I would have said. But what Tricia has taught me is that at least I said *something*. In order for your voice to be influential, you must first have the courage to put your voice out there. Getting it right the first time isn't the goal; the goal is to show up. When I think back on my time with Tricia, what I really see is the capacity that human beings have to grow. The person I am now is not the person I was nearly three years ago when we first met. An influential voice is a voice that is willing to change and transform with time. So today, I am chasing that big dream. I won't be young forever, I acknowledge that mistakes will be made, but I continue to say *something*.

In relation to giving back with financial means, high performers find an organization that they align with and respect and support them. Here are the organizations I give to. These are important to me, but I encourage you to find the ones that resonate with you:

- Kiva, which crowdfunds loans and unlocks capital for the underserved, improving the quality and cost of financial services, and addressing the underlying barriers to financial access around the world. Donations help students pay for tuition, women start businesses, farmers invest in equipment, and families afford needed emergency care.

- Frankie's Friends, which helps save pets' lives by providing grants to assist with the costs of life-saving or life-enhancing emergency or specialty care for pets whose families cannot afford the full cost of treatment; the veterinary costs of certified working dogs; and rehabilitation of sick or injured wildlife.

- ACLU, which works with volunteers and supporters in every corner of the country to defend civil liberties and civil rights through attorneys and activists improving policies and spreading awareness.

- Environmental Defense Fund, which is working every day to cut climate pollution, protect communities threatened by climate change, and develop cost-effective carbon removal strategies.

- Planned Parenthood, which delivers vital reproductive health care, sex education, and information to millions of people worldwide.

- League of Women Voters, which encourages informed and active participation in government, works to increase understanding of major public policy issues, and influences public policy through education and advocacy.

WRITING EXERCISE (LAST CALL!)

What old habit are you willing to exchange for one that is more conducive to your self-improvement?

Let me get you started...

- I'm going to give up pressing the snooze button in exchange for jumping out of bed.
- I'm going to give up coffee dates with people who are taking and set up dates with people who are elevating.
- I'm going to stop canceling my own scheduled work time and commit to keeping the date with myself.

_____

_____

_____

_____

What are ways that you can spend your time more wisely? (Remember that minutes add up. You may be able to rearrange and apply those minutes elsewhere.)

Let me help...

- I can spend more time creating and less time scrolling.
- I can spend more time responding and less time reacting.
- I can spend more time in abundance and less time in lack.

_____

_____

_____

_____

Who do you need to create a boundary around in the interest of being an influential voice?

How about starting with...

- "Thank you for sharing, I'm unavailable for this conversation right now. I'd be happy to have it another time."
- "I appreciate your thoughts on that. It's not something that aligns with me at this time."
- "I'd really appreciate if you would email me. It's my policy to not text with clients."

_____

_____

_____

_____

What systems are in place for communicating and scheduling efficiently?

_____

_____

_____

How are you giving back in knowledge, time, or money?

_____

_____

_____

How will you share your influential voice when you are not on stage?

_____

_____

_____

> ### *Influential Voice Imprints*
>
> An influential voice is generous with gratitude.
>
> Being an influential voice means you embody these values on stage and off.
>
> An influential voice is committed to physical, mental, and emotional health.
>
> Being an influential voice means mindfully giving back of your time and resources.

Conclusion

Say What Matters

> "Words do two major things: they provide
> food for the mind and create light for
> understanding and awareness."
> —*Jim Rohn*

It is my utmost hope that you wholeheartedly feel your influential voice and are clamoring to let it be heard now that you have exclusive training. I know I can't wait to hear what you have to say! The thing about speech, our greatest asset as human beings, is that it can instantly forge connection, emotion, thought, insight, leadership, love, empathy, and impact. Isn't that electrifying?

In all my years doing what I do as a next-level communicator and storyteller, I have learned time and time again that saying what matters does create change. And sometimes, you don't necessarily have time to prep or use the formal training in this book when the moment summons your voice.

A powerful example is Fred Guttenberg, whose fourteen-year-old daughter, Jaime, was killed by a single bullet in the back when she was running for her life at Stoneman Douglas High School on Valentine's Day, 2018. When asked about the importance of speaking out and finding your purpose, he had this to say for *The Influential Voice*: "The moment that defined everything I do wasn't my daughter being murdered—it was the next day when I stood up at a vigil in front of approximately one thousand people. I went to the vigil with my sister and friends. My wife and son didn't go, but I felt that I needed to be around people. When I got there, Christine Hunschofsky, the mayor of Parkland, Florida, asked me to speak. I didn't prepare for it, but I went up there and spoke. It lit me on fire.

"At that speech, I talked about being broken and I was in a really emotional place. I also talked about the realization that my family are victims of gun violence. That night became a defining time that set me on this path of countless speeches, media interviews, and Congressional hearings, even the 2019 State of the Union as Speaker of the House Nancy Pelosi's guest, for what is right: gun reform legislation."

Whatever forum or platform shows itself to you, and it may not be brought on by such profound events like what Fred experienced, please speak. We can't afford any more silence in our world. Your big idea won't simply vanish in time. You're too human, too powerful not to share. If you still hold a limiting belief, I invite you to remember your potential and your competence. These gifts are your birthright. I believe in you. You got this.

And finally, I invite you to declare out loud once more today, again tomorrow, and on into the next day, "What I have to say matters. My voice matters." By speaking this out loud, you are taking an oath to yourself, to the Universe, and to all the collective voices everywhere. You have stepped into the role of being the influential voice.

References

Alison, Jane. "Beyond the Narrative Arc." *The Paris Review*. March 27, 2019.
https://www.theparisreview.org/blog/2019/03/27/beyond-the-narrative-arc/.

Antoniacci, Mandy. "Looking Up in an Epidemic of Looking Down." TEDxLincoln-Square. March 2018.
https://www.ted.com/talks/
mandy_antoniacci_looking_up_in_an_epidemic_of_looking_down.

Brown, Brené. "The Power of Vulnerability." TEDxHouston. 2010.
https://www.ted.com/talks/brene_brown_the_power_of_vulnerability

Clement, J. "Number of e-mails per day worldwide 2017–2023." Statista. August 9, 2019.
https://www.statista.com/statistics/456500/daily-number-of-e-mails-worldwide/.

Culwell-Block, Logan. "16 Most-Revived Musicals in Broadway History Since 1927."
Playbill. August 13, 2020.
https://www.playbill.com/
article/16-most-revived-musicals-in-broadway-history-since-1927.

Daley, Beth. "Donald Trump's 'Chinese Virus': the Politics of Naming." The Conversation. April 21, 2020.
https://theconversation.com/donald-trumps-chinese-virus-the-politics-of-naming-136796.

Dispenza, Joe. *Breaking the Habit of Being Yourself*. New York: Hay House, Inc., 2013.

"A Brief History of Drepung Loseling Monastery."
http://www.drepung.org/changing/mystical/Monast.htm.

Dunckley, MD, Victoria L. "Screentime Is Making Kids Moody, Crazy, and Lazy."
Psychology Today. August 18, 2015.

https://www.psychologytoday.com/us/blog/mental-wealth/201508/
screentime-is-making-kids-moody-crazy-and-lazy.

Dweck, Carol. "Teaching a Growth Mindset." Stanford/YouTube. November 3, 2015.
https://www.youtube.com/watch?v=isHM1rEd3GE.

Equal Rights Amendment. Equalrightsamendment.org. Alice Paul Institute.
https://www.equalrightsamendment.org.

Fox, Margalit. "Toni Morrison, Towering Novelist of the Black Experience, Dies at 88."
New York Times. August 6, 2019.
https://www.nytimes.com/2019/08/06/books/toni-morrison-dead.html.

Friedman, Kristen. "Cinderella Tales and Their Significance." University at Albany, State
University of New York Scholars Archive.
https://scholarsarchive.library.albany.edu/cgi/viewcontent.
cgi?article=1001&context=honorscollege_anthro.

Fritze, John. "Trump Used Words Like 'Invasion' and 'Killer' to Discuss Immigrants at
Rallies 500 Times: USA TODAY Analysis." *USA Today.* August 8, 2019.
https://www.usatoday.com/story/news/politics/elections/2019/08/08/
trump-immigrants-rhetoric-criticized-el-paso-dayton-shootings/1936742001/.

Gilbert, Elizabeth. *Committed.* New York: Riverhead Books, 2011.

"Can Hypnosis Help You..." Grace Space Hypnosis.
https://gshypnosis.com.

Griffith, Janelle. "Ahmaud Arbery Shooting: A Timeline of the Case." *NBC
News.* May 11, 2020.
https://www.nbcnews.com/news/us-news/
ahmaud-arbery-shooting-timeline-case-n1204306.

Harris, Tristan. "How a Handful of Tech Companies Control Billions of Minds Every
Day." TED2017. April 2017.
https://www.ted.com/talks/tristan_harris_how_a_handful_of_tech_companies_con-
trol_billions_of_minds_every_day?language=en.

Hollman, Rich. "How Improv Training Can Create Compassionate Behavior." TEDxLincolnSquare. May 4, 2017.
https://www.youtube.com/watch?v=KcrbEQkTAvk.

Honnold, Alex. Website.
http://www.alexhonnold.com.

Humphrey, Doris, Barbara Pollack, and Stuyvesant Van Veen. *The Art of Making Dances.* New York: Princeton Book Company, August 1991.

Hylton, Jeremy. "The Complete Works of William Shakespeare." Maintained by *The Tech*/MIT.
http://shakespeare.mit.edu.

Jensen, Antesa. Website.
http://www.antesajensen.com/about-antesa.

Laskowski, MD, Edward. "What Are the Risks of Sitting Too Much?" Mayo Clinic.
https://www.mayoclinic.org/healthy-lifestyle/adult-health/expert-answers/sitting/faq-20058005.

Malandro, Loretta. *Speak Up, Show Up, and Stand Out.* New York: McGraw-Hill Education, 2014.

Mather, Victor. "FIFA President Proposes Expansion of Women's World Cup and Doubling of Prize Money." *New York Times.* July 5, 2019.
https://www.nytimes.com/2019/07/05/sports/fifa-world-cup-expansion.html.

Maxwell, John. "Want Better Relationships? Be Relatable!" John Maxwell Blog. May 21, 2019.
https://www.johnmaxwell.com/blog/want-better-relationships-be-relatable/.

Milk, Harvey. "The Hope Speech." *Figures of Speech.* Almeida University. June 25, 1978.
https://www.speech.almeida.co.uk/harvey-milk.

Montana, Sarah. Website.
https://www.sarahmontana.com.

Neagle, David. *The Millions Within.* New York: Morgan James Publishing, 2013.

Read, Bridget. "What We Know About the Killing of Breonna Taylor." *The Cut.* July 9, 2020; updated September 29, 2020.
https://www.thecut.com/2020/07/breonna-taylor-louisville-shooting-police-what-we-know.html.

Robbins, Liz. "'We Have to Be Better': Megan Rapinoe and the Year of Victory and Advocacy." *New York Times.* December 18, 2019; updated November 6, 2020.

https://www.nytimes.com/2019/12/18/sports/year-of-victory-advocacy.html.

Sax, Sarah. "New York City Needs to Better Regulate Noise." *City & State New York.* December 4, 2019. https://www.cityandstateny.com/articles/opinion/opinion/new-york-city-needs-better-regulate-noise.html.

Siang, Yu Teo. "How to Create Engaging UX Case Studies with Freytag's 5-Part Dramatic Structure." Interaction Design Foundation. July 20, 2020. https://www.interaction-design.org/literature/article/how-to-create-engaging-ux-case-studies-with-freytag-s-5-part-dramatic-structure.

Smedley, Kristin. "Kristin's Causes." http://kristinsmedley.com/about/kristins-causes/.

____. "How I learned to see through the eyes of my sons." TEDxLincoln-Square. May 4, 2017. https://www.youtube.com/watch?v=Rdar-vklzeE.

Sternlicht, Alexandra. "Famished NYC Rats Are Harassing Outdoor Diners." *Forbes.* July 10, 2020. https://www.forbes.com/sites/alexandrasternlicht/2020/07/10/famished-nyc-rats-are-harassing-outdoor-diners/#7f3f73bc11d2.

Stoker, Dacre, and J. D. Barker. "Bram Stoker Claimed That Parts of *Dracula* Were Real. Here's What We Know About the Story Behind the Novel." *Time.* October 3, 2018. https://time.com/5411826/bram-stoker-dracula-history/.

StoryCorps. https://storycorps.org.

Suciu, Peter. "Twitter Has Changed How World Leaders Can Communicate and May Have Stopped a War." *Forbes.* January 9, 2020. https://www.forbes.com/sites/petersuciu/2020/01/09/twitter-has-changed-how-world-leaders-can-communicate-and-may-have-stopped-a-war/#58f824c28391.

TEDx Program. https://www.ted.com/about/programs-initiatives/tedx-program

Toastmasters International website. https://www.toastmasters.org.

United Nations. "Population."

https://www.un.org/en/sections/issues-depth/population/.

Withnall, Adam. "Are You Braver Than the Average Briton? UK's Top 13 Fears Revealed."

Independent. March 24, 2014.

https://www.independent.co.uk/news/uk/home-news/are-you-braver-than-the-average-briton-uks-top-13-fears-revealed-9212346.html.

Acknowledgments

There have been many influential voices in my life over the years. They have all played a starring role in the development of who I've become in the world. I'm deeply thankful to all of you. First, my dance teacher and dear friend for more than forty years, Sharon McGuire. Your demands, coupled with belief, showed me no limitations. Kay Henderson, the chair and modern dance professor at Stephens College, who believed in me and gave me a scholarship more than once, empowering me to step fully into my truth. Michael Simms, who gave me the starring role in the ballet he choreographed, which taught me I was a soloist through and through. Dancer great, Christopher Gillis, my mentor from Paul Taylor, who saw in me what I could not. Lisa Wheeler, my dance sister and life contemporary who influences me on and off the stage. Karen Graham, friend and another dance sister, your voice like a powerful whisper has guided me often on stage and off. Karen Graham, friend and another dance sister, your voice like a powerful whisper has guided me often on stage and off. Petra Kolber, who asked me to direct her TEDx, which started this avalanche of abundance. Heather Hamilton, who's been my muse and friend and has given an influential voice through movement again and again. Michael Roderick, a mentor and trusted friend who always speaks the truth for good. Jamie Broderick, who stood with me and beside me and taught me what I didn't know. Mari Carmen Pizarro, a woman whose friendship, leadership, and power lifts me up daily. Emily and James Williams, my coaches, mentors, and friends, who shined a light on my work and my essence and reminded me anything is possible. And I do mean anything. Candi Cross, my friend and collaborator in all things big voices and big talks. Finally, my husband, Joe. Your influential voice has taught me more than I sometimes desired to learn, more than I ever thought I could love, and your belief in me and respect for me make this journey bigger than I could ever imagine.

About the Author

Tricia Brouk is an international award-winning director. She has worked in theater, film, and television for three decades. Her work includes the writing of two musicals, both produced in New York City, a one-woman show, and four documentaries, two eligible for Academy of Motion Picture Arts and Sciences nominations. She had an extensive career as a dancer performing all over the world. In addition to her work in the entertainment industry, Tricia applies her expertise to the art of public speaking. She was the executive producer of Speakers Who Dare and TEDxLincolnSquare and now The Big Talk Live. She has shepherded more than fifty speakers onto more than fifteen TEDx stages in under three years. She is currently being featured in a new documentary called *Big Stages*, which highlights the transformation of her speakers. Tricia's commitment and devotion to inclusion is a priority as all of her shows, events, and communities are diverse.

She curates and hosts the Speaker Salon in NYC, *The Big Talk*, an award-winning podcast on iTunes and YouTube. She directed and produced *The Big Talk Over Dinner: Race and Immigration* that premiered at the Be Your Best Self Expo in 2020. She was awarded Top Director of 2019 by the International Association of Top Professionals and is relentless about her vision of amplifying voices all over the world.

Tricia lives in New York City with her husband, Joe Ricci, and their two cats, Lola and Bella. Their building faces the Alvin Ailey Dance Theater, where she gets to watch young dancers realize their dreams every single day.